T0223832

HCI Design Knowledge
Critique, Challenge, and a Way Forward

Synthesis Lectures on Human-Centered Informatics

Editor
John M. Carroll, *Penn State University*

Human-Centered Informatics (HCI) is the intersection of the cultural, the social, the cognitive, and the aesthetic with computing and information technology. It encompasses a huge range of issues, theories, technologies, designs, tools, environments, and human experiences in knowledge work, recreation and leisure activity, teaching and learning, and the potpourri of everyday life. The series publishes state-of-the-art syntheses, case studies, and tutorials in key areas. It shares the focus of leading international conferences in HCI.

HCI Design Knowledge: Critique, Challenge, and a Way Forward
John Long, Steve Cummaford, and Adam Stork

Disability Interactions: Creating Inclusive Innovations
Catherine Holloway and Giulia Barbareschi

Participatory Design
Susanne Bødker, Christian Dindler, Ole S. Iversen, and Rachel C. Smith

The Trouble With Sharing: Interpersonal Challenges in Peer-to-Peer Exchange
Airi Lampinen

Interface for an App—The Design Rationale Leading to an App that Allows Someone With Type 1 Diabetes to Self-Manage Their Condition
Bob Spence

Organizational Implementation: The Design in Use of Information Systems
Morten Hertzum

Data-Driven Personas
Bernard J. Jansen, Joni Salminen, Soon-gyo Jung, and Kathleen Guan

Worth-Focused Design, Book 2: Approaches, Context, and Case Studies
Gilbert Cockton

Common Ground in Electronically Mediated Conversation

Andrew Monk

© Springer Nature Switzerland AG 2022
Reprint of original edition © Morgan & Claypool 2022

All rights reserved. No part of this publication may be reproduced, stored in a retrieval system, or transmitted in any form or by any means—electronic, mechanical, photocopy, recording, or any other except for brief quotations in printed reviews, without the prior permission of the publisher.

HCI Design Knowledge: Critique, Challenge, and a Way Forward
John Long, Steve Cummaford, Adam Stork

ISBN: 978-3-031-79197-0 Paperback
ISBN: 978-3-031-79209-0 PDF
ISBN: 978-3-031-79221-2 Hardcover

DOI 10.1007/978-3-031-79209-0

A Publication in the Springer series
SYNTHESIS LECTURES ON HUMAN-CENTERED INFORMATICS

Lecture #54
Series Editor: John M. Carroll, Penn State University

Series ISSN 1946-7680 Print 1946-7699 Electronic

HCI Design Knowledge

Critique, Challenge, and a Way Forward

John Long
University College, London

Steve Cummaford
Ted Baker

Adam Stork
Concerto

SYNTHESIS LECTURES ON HUMAN-CENTERED INFORMATICS #54

ABSTRACT

This is the first of two books concerned with engineering design principles for Human-Computer Interaction-Engineering Design Principles (HCI-EDPs). The book presents the background for the companion volume. The background is divided into three parts and comprises—"HCI for EDPs," "HCI Design Knowledge for EDPs," and "HCI-EDPs—A Way Forward for HCI Design Knowledge." The companion volume reports in full the acquisition of initial HCI-EDPs in the domains of domestic energy planning and control and business-to-consumer electronic commerce (Long, Cummaford, and Stork, 2022, in press).

The background includes the disciplinary basis for HCI-EDPs, a critique of, and the challenge for, HCI design knowledge in general. The latter is categorised into three types for the purposes in hand. These are craft artefacts and design practice experience, models and methods, and principles, rules, and heuristics. HCI-EDPs attempt to meet the challenge for HCI design knowledge by increasing the reliability of its fitness-for-purpose to support HCI design practice. The book proposes "instance-first/class-first" approaches to the acquisition of HCI-EDPs. The approaches are instantiated in two case studies, summarised here and reported in full in the companion volume.

The book is for undergraduate students trying to understand the different kinds of HCI design knowledge, their varied and associated claims, and their potential for application to design practice now and in the future. The book also provides grounding for young researchers seeking to develop further HCI-EDPs in their own work.

KEYWORDS

HCI engineering design principles; HCI-EDPs; HCI design knowledge; craft artefacts and design practice experience; models and methods; principles, rules, and heuristics; HCI design knowledge critique and challenge; HCI-EDP reliability and fitness-for-purpose

Contents

Preface

ABOUT THIS BOOK

The book is one of two. The companion volume is entitled *Towards Engineering Design Principles for HCI* (Long et al., 2022, in press).

The title of the present book describes its scope and content. The general scope is human-computer interaction design knowledge. Its general content comprises HCI design knowledge as craft artefacts and design practice experience, models and methods, and principles, rules, and heuristics. The specific scope is engineering design principles for HCI (HCI-EDPs). Its specific content comprises initial, as opposed to final, HCI-EDPs for the domains of domestic energy planning and control and business-to-consumer electronic commerce. The latter are summarised in this book and reported fully in the companion volume.

The present book is divided into three parts. The first is "HCI for HCI-EDPs." It presents the conceptions required and applied in the case studies of the acquisition of initial HCI-EDPs. The second part is "HCI Design Knowledge for HCI-EDPs." It presents the HCI design knowledge required and applied in the case studies of initial HCI-EDPs. The third part is "EDPs—A Way Forward for HCI Design Knowledge." It summarises the two case studies reporting the acquisition of initial HCI-EDPs in the domains of domestic energy planning and control and business-to-customer electronic commerce. The book references other types of HCI design knowledge by way of exemplification and contrast. Such HCI design knowledge, although not used in the present case studies, could be used in the form of "best-practice" in any future acquisition of HCI-EDPs.

HCI design knowledge is at the heart of HCI. Its acquisition is the object of HCI research. Its application is the object of HCI practice. The development of both over the years has been extensive. The latter is attested both by the HCI research literature and by HCI reporting, at conferences such as the CHI series.

This undisputed development, however, has failed, with to address the fundamental question of the fitness-for-purpose of design knowledge from an HCI discipline perspective. With few exceptions, there is little criticism of design knowledge from a discipline perspective. This is opposed to its propagation and development more generally, in the research and professional literature. This book provides such a disciplinary perspective and an associated critique.

The latter constitutes a challenge for HCI design knowledge in general. To be fit-for-purpose, an HCI discipline requires design knowledge to be reliable in its application to design and its reliability to be known explicitly. Further, its reliability needs to be demonstrated, so creating the potential for disciplinary consensus, as required by a discipline. At present, there is no such guarantee, absolute or relative, that its application to the design of interactive systems to satisfy user and other requirements as desired, has the effect claimed for it. An HCI discipline requires such claims to be explicit. In general, current claims are implicit. Design knowledge, then, is not known to be effective from an HCI discipline perspective.

Some general thoughts are offered on the way forward for the different types of HCI design knowledge described and the associated developments and movements. In contrast, a specific proposal is made, concerning the way forward, as HCI-EDPs.

The book sets out "instance-first/class-first" approaches to the acquisition of HCI-EDPs. The approach is instantiated in two case studies, summarised here and reported in full in the companion volume (Long et al., 2022, in press). The application domains of the case studies are domestic energy planning and control, and business-to-consumer electronic commerce. Both studies report the acquisition of initial, as opposed to final, HCI-EDPs. Both reports include—an introduction to HCI-EDPs, two cycles of their development, their presentation, and assessment and identification of further HCI-EDP research.

There is a need for both books. Much has been claimed for current HCI design knowledge and rightly so. Its propagation and influence is well attested by the HCI literature and CHI conference reports. New developments and movements continue its advance. However, a critical review of HCI design knowledge, from a disciplinary perspective, is timely and welcome. The resulting critique, however, attempts to be transparent, balanced, and proportionate. It makes explicit the criteria, which are applied and their rationale. The criteria and critique apply to all the types of HCI design knowledge, including that of HCI-EDPs, the way forward, proposed here.

A search of the HCI literature suggests "instance-first/class-first" approaches to the acquisition of HCI-EDPs to be novel with the exception of "design patterns." There is overlap of HCI-EDPs with the latter, but also differences. Carrying forward the former is considered to carry forward the latter, at least to a first approximation.

The review of HCI design knowledge from a discipline perspective suggests the absence of, and so the need for, more effective support for HCI design practice. Practice assignments, at the end of each chapter, facilitate the understanding of HCI design knowledge in general, including HCI-EDPs in particular. The final chapter suggests the future research required for acquiring further such HCI-EDPs.

ABOUT THE RATIONALE

The publication of the two books attempts to fill a gap in the literature. First, a review of HCI design knowledge from a disciplinary perspective. Second, HCI-EDPs as a way forward from that perspective.

The books differ from other recent books concerning HCI design knowledge and its application, such as Ritter, Baxter, and Churchill *Foundations for Designing User-Centered Systems* (2014); Hartson and Pyla *The UX Book: Agile UX Design for a Quality User Experience* (2018); Kim *Human-Computer Interaction—Foundations and Practice* (2020), and Zagalo *Engagement Design: Designing for Interaction Motivations* (2020). The present book conceives HCI design knowledge from a discipline perspective. The companion volume instantiates HCI-EDPs as a way forward from that perspective. Taken together, the two books constitute a contrast with the books referenced.

The books also differ from Long's *Approaches and Frameworks for HCI Research* (2021). He proposes an approach and a framework for HCI engineering research, along with other types of research. Also, he refers, by way of an associated design research exemplar, to specific and general HCI principles. However, Long presents no critique of the different types of design knowledge, other than for the purposes of their formulation as approaches and frameworks. Neither does he report any case studies of their acquisition. The present books, then, can best be understood as starting, where Long left off.

ABOUT THE AUTHORS

The authors feel able to write such a book. They developed the critique of HCI design knowledge, during their time at University College London. It has been used to frame and to support related research, of which two case study examples are summarised here and reported fully in the companion volume (Long et al., 2022, in press). The authors' engagement with the area of HCI design knowledge research is attested by key publications, which are referenced throughout the book—Stork (1999), Cummaford (2007), and Long (2010 and 2021). The authors continue to engage with developments in HCI design knowledge and its application, along with the domains of domestic energy planning and control, and business-to-consumer electronic commerce, respectively.

Long was the initiator of the work and thesis director of studies for both the Stork and the Cummaford theses and associated case studies. He also wrote the first version of all the remaining chapters. He is responsible with Springer for bringing the book to publication. For these reasons, Long appears as first author. Cummaford and Stork are ordered alphabetically. All chapters have been reviewed and revised by all authors.

ABOUT THE READERSHIP

The book is primarily for graduate and postgraduate students and in particular those studying HCI. It is also for young academic researchers and their directors of studies, interested in acquiring grounding in HCI-EDPs and in developing them further. Also in developing any other type of validatable and validated HCI design knowledge, as a way forward. Practice assignments at the end of each chapter support students in understanding, articulating, and applying the concepts presented.

The book is also of interest to researchers and practitioners in related areas, contributing to HCI design knowledge, either directly or indirectly. The areas include cognitive psychology, human factors, design research, software engineering, design science, cognitive ergonomics, UX-design, and human-centred informatics. They all provide an appropriate readership for the book, its critique, its challenge, and its way forward.

Acknowledgments

The book is offered as a tribute to colleagues and PhD students at the EU/UCL Unit at University College London, whose earlier research contributions have made it possible (for more information about such research contributions, see hciengineering.net).

Thanks are due to Jack Carroll for including the book in his Synthesis Lectures on Human-centred Informatics Series, to Diane Cerra and Christine Kiilerich for faultless editing, and Deb Gabriel as compositor, in bringing the book to print. Thanks are also due to two anonymous reviewers, who have contributed to improving the clarity and coverage of an earlier draft.

Dedication

To our families and friends for their support, patience, and understanding.

Terminology

Agile Methods

Air Traffic Management (ATM)
    Cognitive Design Problem
    Flight Progress Strip (FPS)
    Planning Horizon
    Theory of Planning Horizon (TOPH)

Apple
    Lisa
    Macintosh

Applied Psychology

Approaches

Best-Practice Design

Best Selling Lists

Civil Engineering

Class-based Human-Computer Interaction
- Engineering Design Principles (HCI-EDPs)
    Strategy
    Design Problem
    Design Solution

Cognitive Engineering

Cognitive Ergonomics

Cognitive Psychology

Computer Architecture

Conceptions
    HCI-EDPs
    HCI Class Design Problem
    HCI Class Design Solution
    HCI General Design Problem
    HCI General Design Solution
    HCI Specific Design Problem

    HCI Specific Design Solution

Costs Matrix
    Structures
    Behaviours

Craft Artefacts and Design Experience

Design Knowledge
    Challenge
    Critique
    Design Problem
    Design Solution
    Heuristics
    Principles
    Rules
    Way Forward

Design Research

Design Science

Direct Manipulation Theory

Domain

Domestic Energy
    Case Study

Discipline
    Applied
    Craft
    Engineering
    HCI
    Innovation
    Science

Ease of Use

Ecological Theory

E-Commerce

Effective Support for Design

PART I

HCI for HCI Engineering Design Principles

The first part of the book presents the conceptions required and applied in the case studies of the acquisition of initial HCI-EDPs from a discipline perspective. The conceptions comprise those for HCI, HCI design, HCI knowledge, and HCI design knowledge. Other types of HCI design knowledge are referenced in the individual chapters by way of exemplification and contrast. Such HCI design knowledge was not used in the present case studies. However, it could be used as best-practice in any future acquisition of HCI-EDPs.

CHAPTER 1

HCI

SUMMARY

This chapter introduces Human-Computer Interaction (HCI) and its current state. HCI is conceived from a discipline perspective. The HCI discipline comprises an HCI general problem, with a particular HCI scope, which conducts HCI research. The latter acquires and validates HCI design knowledge to support HCI design practice. The conception supports the acquisition of initial HCI-EDPs, as summarised in Chapter 9 and reported fully in the companion volume (Long et al., 2022, in press). Other discipline conceptions are referenced in contrast. The introduction forms the basis for the following chapter on HCI design.

1.1 DISCIPLINE

The discipline, assumed here for the acquisition of HCI-EDPs, comprises a general problem and a particular scope (see Long, 2021). For example, the discipline of science has the general problem of understanding natural phenomena. Psychology, as a sub-discipline of science, has the particular scope of understanding human behaviour. In turn, understanding natural phenomena comprises the practices of explaining known phenomena and predicting unknown phenomena. The explanation, together with the prediction of natural phenomena, constitute the scientific understanding of such phenomena.

The discipline, assumed here, further comprises practices and the knowledge required to support them. Research acquires and validates such knowledge. For example, scientific theory is the knowledge supporting the practices of explanation and prediction and so the scientific understanding of natural phenomena.

Last, the discipline can be assessed for the appropriateness of its knowledge to support its practices in terms of the former's completeness, coherence and fitness-for-purpose, and other criteria.

No conception of HCI, as a discipline, meets with general acceptance at this time. This includes the conception proposed here. Nor is general acceptance required for present purposes. Different conceptions exist from different perspectives, for different purposes, with different values and can be assessed by different criteria. However, it should be noted, that the present conception shares many assumptions with both scientific, engineering, and other types of discipline, as presented in books, such as for example, Harper et al. (2008) and Rogers, Sharp, and Preece (2011).

1.2   HCI DISCIPLINE

The HCI discipline, as assumed here for the purpose of acquiring initial HCI-EDPs, identifies itself as a specific field of academic study. The HCI discipline comprises a general HCI problem and an HCI particular scope. The relationship is shown in Figure 1.1.

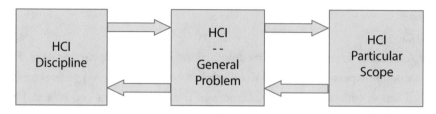

Figure 1.1: HCI discipline.

Although the figure serves its purpose, its format serves a more general aim, which is to support comparison with other such figures, for example, those of Figures 2–8.1. The format helps identify the similarities and differences, as concerns the conceptual contents. Likewise, for alternative conceptions, which readers might like to formulate for themselves.

The conceptions of the HCI discipline may take different forms for different purposes and to embody different values. An example is Long's (2021) categorisation of approaches and frameworks for HCI as innovation, art, craft, engineering, applied, and science. Further, according to Rogers (2012), there are six overlapping fields, in addition to HCI—ubiquitous computing, human factors, cognitive engineering, cognitive ergonomics, computer-supported cooperative work (CSCW), and information systems. She goes on to claim that the following seven academic disciplines may contribute to these overlapping fields—ergonomics, psychology/cognitive psychology, design informatics, engineering, computer science/software engineering, and social science.

This is without the so-called "movements," such as "design science" (Hevner et al., 2004), "design research" (Roedl and Stolterman, 2013), and "agile methods" (da Silva et al., 2015; Gothelf and Seiden, 2016).

These different approaches and frameworks, overlapping fields, academic disciples, and movements may have their own conceptions of HCI, which may be appropriate for their own application. However, they are not the conceptions underlying the present quest for HCI-EDPs. According to the latter, the HCI discipline general problem is the design of interactive human-computer systems to satisfy user and other requirements. The design of human-computer interactive systems can take many forms, for example, simulation and implementation at their most general. More specific forms of design are embodied in storyboard scenarios, wire-frame models, prototypes, and initial system versions.

The HCI particular scope of the HCI discipline general problem of design is humans interacting with computers to do something as desired. What is desired is usually by the users, but may also be by the systems developers, the commissioners of the system and indeed a range of other possible interested third parties. Both users and computers can be characterised in different ways for the purposes of such design, for example the professional user, the occasional user and the older user. An instance of the design of human-computer interactions to do something as desired by users and system commissioners might be the initial prototype of a portable interactive on-line dating system or Version 1 of a new gaming platform.

HCI discipline research, as conceived by HCI-EDP acquisition and validation comprises the diagnosis of design problems and the prescription of design solutions, as they relate to performance. HCI research acquires and validates HCI design knowledge to support HCI design practices. Other conceptions, as cited earlier, have other perspectives on research.

The latter can take many forms, for example, observational study, laboratory experiment, and model/method development. Knowledge acquisition may involve different criteria, for example, completeness, need, coherence, viability, risk, profitability, and fitness-for-purpose. An instance of research might be the application of face recognition to the checking of traveller identity at national boundaries.

HCI discipline knowledge is acquired and validated to support HCI design practices. Knowledge may be of different kinds, for example, design methods, design heuristics, and design guidelines. Knowledge may be more-or-less formal, for example, HCI-EDPs and as embodied in successful design artefacts, respectively. Knowledge may also offer more-or-less guaranteed support in terms of reliability of application, for example, HCI-EDPs and design heuristics, respectively. An instance of research might be the production of guidelines or models for the development of trust in on-line banking transactions.

HCI discipline practices are supported by knowledge, acquired and validated by research. Design practices include, for example, specifying and implementing human-computer interactions for interactive systems to do something as desired. Users of an interactive on-line shopping system might complain that they cannot manage their shopping budget well enough. They are unable to keep track of the cost of the goods in their shopping cart and so spend more than they intend. Were this considered a user problem and a design problem, design practice might determine a solution in the form of a display of the running total of the cost of the scanned goods in the users' cart, as a percentage of their pre-entered budget. The solution might then be specified and implemented. The solution might also satisfy a business need for users to be able to sustain a realistic spend threshold, rather than one, which is too low, resulting in lower sales and profits. For a more detailed exemplification of HCI as a disciple, consider the two case studies, summarised in Chapter 9.

The domestic energy planning and control case study (see § 9.1 and Figure 1.1) espouses the HCI discipline, with its own specific field of academic study, as engineering. The latter discipline has the general problem of the design of domestic energy planning and control interactive systems. The particular scope comprises home occupiers, interacting with devices for the planning, and controlling of house temperatures, as desired. The case study is itself an example of HCI research. The business-to-consumer electronic commerce case study (see § 9.2 and Figure 1.1) also espouses the HCI discipline, with its own specific field of academic study, as engineering. The latter discipline has the general problem of the design of business-to-consumer electronic commerce interactive systems. The particular scope comprises buyers, interacting with computers to acquire goods, as desired. The case study is itself an example of HCI research.

In both case studies, the HCI discipline espoused is for the purposes if acquiring HCI-EDPs. Other conceptions of HCI as a discipline, identified earlier, may be espoused for other purposes and with other values.

1.2.1   HCI GENERAL PROBLEM

The HCI general problem, as assumed here for the purpose of acquiring initial HCI-EDPs, comprises a general description and its state.

1.2.1.1 GENERAL

The HCI general problem is one of design. As an example of HCI design, the graphical user interface (GUI) resulted from designs originating with Xerox, Apple, and other research and development organisations. GUI interfaces currently characterise the design of applications, such as multi-media learning, e-commerce, and Internet banking. Other application designs range from buying pet insurance, to on-line dating, flower arranging, and exercising at home. Public service application designs characterise the control panels, used by aviation and rail services.

The HCI general problem of design is also reflected in the activities of HCI designers and researchers. Applied psychologists seek to understand applications both theoretically and empirically. Cognitive engineers model the knowledge, required to use interactive systems. Ease of use specialists evaluate the usability of applications. Design science researchers characterise different types of design and associate them with different types of risk. Human-centred designers assess user and other requirements against application system functions. Last, interaction researchers model task behaviours using wireframe and other models.

1.2.1.2 STATE OF HCI GENERAL PROBLEM

The state of the HCI general problem, as one of design, is described in terms of the progress made in the design of applications. HCI design can be characterised, as a set of practices, comprising graphic, product, artist, industrial, and film industry design (Rogers, 2012). Graphic design has progressed from static images to animations in support of the illustration and attention seeking, required by commercial advertising. Product design has progressed from drawing board to interactive computer-aided design of buildings and domestic artefacts, such as furniture and fabrics. Artist design has progressed from paper-based sketching to interactive systems, supporting painting and drawing. Industrial design has progressed from interactive to part-automated systems for manufactured artefacts, such as spare parts and tools. Last, film industry design has progressed from voice to synthesised voice and image representations to be found in social media videos.

For a more detailed exemplification of the HCI general problem, consider the two case studies, summarised in Chapter 9.

The domestic energy planning and control case study (see § 9.1 and Figure 1.1) has the general problem of the design of domestic energy planning and control interactive systems, comprising the specification and implementation of such systems. The latter have the particular scope of home occupiers, interacting with devices for the planning and controlling of house temperatures, as desired. The case study is itself an example of HCI research.

The business-to-consumer electronic commerce case study (see § 9.2 and Figure 1.1) has the general problem of the design of the business-to-consumer electronic commerce interactive systems, comprising the specification and implementation of such systems. The latter have the particular scope of buyers, interacting with computers to acquire goods, as desired. The case study is itself an example of HCI research.

Progress, then, has been made by design practices, which solve the HCI general problem of design.

1.2.2   HCI PARTICULAR SCOPE

The HCI particular scope, as assumed here for the purpose of acquiring initial HCI-EDPs, comprises a general description and its state.

1.2.2.1 GENERAL

For acquiring HCI-EDPs, it is assumed that the particular scope of the HCI general problem is design of humans interacting with computers to do something as desired (see also Long, 2021). What is desired is expressed as performance, whether in terms of user experience or the outcomes of the interaction. The latter may also reflect both those of the user and those of the application provider. The particular scope of Internet banking applications is the support of bank customers to pay bills, to make money transfers and to keep a record of their savings, consistent with their financial needs and goals and with those of the banks, such as profitability. The particular scope of multi-media applications is support for the sharing of communications and images among family and friends, according to their individual preferences and in line with the business interests of the hosting platform. Last, the particular scope of smart 'phone central heating applications is to support the setting of ambient room temperatures. The latter are set according to the time of year and the comfort requirements of the house occupiers, even when they are not themselves at home and according to the profit criteria of the suppliers.

The HCI particular scope of humans interacting with computers to do something as desired is also reflected in the activities of HCI designers and researchers of applications. This is the case for applied psychologists, design scientists, cognitive engineers, design researchers, ease of use/usability experts, human-centred design consultants, and user experience (UX) design practitioners. However, although espousing different approaches to design and research, all address the same HCI particular scope.

1.2.2.2 STATE OF HCI PARTICULAR SCOPE

The state of the particular scope of the HCI general problem is described in terms of humans interacting with computers to do something as desired. The state comprises, for example, humans, computers, interactions, and performance. The progress in the state of each follows.

The progress in the scope of humans can be characterised, as expanding sets of users, for example, professional, office and factory, domestic, young, and older users (Harper et al., 2008). Professional users, for example, include scientists and engineers, using project-planning applications to monitor project progress and budgets. Office and factory users include managers and supervisors, using spreadsheet and PowerPoint applications to organise staff rotas. Domestic users include family and friends, engaging with communications and multi-media applications to maintain social relations, even when apart. Young users include children, using educational and gaming applications to support their evolving engagement with society and with the world at large. Last, older users include the retired, using social support and medical applications to maintain their quality of life.

The progress in the scope of computers can also be described, as expanding sets of computing technology, for example, mainframe, personal, communicating, and ubiquitous (Sharp, Rogers, and Preece, 2007). Mainframe computers are located in a single place and serve the application needs of individual organisations, such as commercial companies, hospital trusts, and military centres. Personal computers are located with individuals, and so are to be found everywhere, serving the application needs of managers, housewives, secretaries, the retired, and supervisors. Communicating computers may be located anywhere, serving the application needs of geographically distributed companies, such as global suppliers and families, whose members live in different countries. Last, ubiquitous computers are located everywhere, serving the application needs of people, whether at home, at work, elsewhere, travelling to the office and factory, or on holiday at home or abroad.

The progress in the scope of interactions can be described, as expanding sets of interactions, for example, punching cards, typing programmes, issuing command-based instructions, pointing, touching, speaking, and gesturing (Rogers et al., 2011). Punching cards involves making holes in paper cards, which can then be "read" by a computer. Typing programmes involves instructing the computer in a technical language. Issuing command-based instructions involves the technical use of ordinary language. Pointing usually involves a cursor, controlled by a mouse. Touching typically requires the human finger and a display. Speaking involves the human voice and usually ordinary language. Last, gesturing involves the hands or other parts of the human body.

The progress in the scope of "doing something as desired" as performance can be characterised historically in terms of the concept's development. For example, performance was initially expressed as speed and errors, reflecting the time taken to complete a task and the number of errors committed in so doing. Desired performance might then be expressed for air traffic controllers as "errorless performance," for example as reflected by the absence of safety violations. A trade-off was found to exist between the two concepts. The faster a task is performed, the more errors are likely to be committed and vice versa. Effective performance as optimisation describes a task, as being done as well as it is possible to do so. Desired performance might then be expressed for production workers, as "optimal performance," for example, as reflected by workflow criteria. Later, some researchers rejected effectiveness as an inappropriate performance criterion for play, leisure, and education (conceived as opposed to work). The concept of performance was subsequently extended to include emotional engagement, as instanced by the performance of tasks, affording "fun," such as in gaming, puzzle-solving, and pet-caring applications.

For a more detailed exemplification of the HCI particular scope, consider the two case studies, summarised in Chapter 9 (also Long et al., 2022, in press).

The domestic energy planning and control case study (see § 9.1 and Figure 1.1) has the general problem of the design of energy planning and control interactive systems, comprising the specification and implementation of such systems. The latter have the particular scope of home occupiers, interacting with devices for the planning and controlling of their comfort preference, as desired. The case study is itself an example of HCI research.

The business-to-consumer electronic commerce case study (see § 9.2 and Figure 1.1) has the general problem of the design of the business-to-consumer electronic commerce interactive systems, comprising the specification and implementation of such systems. The latter have the particular scope of buyers, interacting with computers to acquire physical goods, such as tea and information goods, such as alarm alerts, as desired. The case study is itself an example of HCI research.

1.2.3   HCI RESEARCH

HCI research, as assumed here for the purpose of acquiring initial HCI-EDPs, comprises a general description and its state.

1.2.3.1 GENERAL

HCI research acquires and validates HCI knowledge to support practices in solving the general HCI problem of design with the particular scope of humans interacting with computers to do something as desired.

Internet banking research has concerned itself with ways of identifying customers' requirements to support the design of novel interfaces for managing, that is planning and controlling, their financial affairs, together with the interests of the bank, such as safety. Multi-media research has concerned itself with understanding the sharing of communications and images among colleagues and customers to produce guidelines in support of multi-media video design. Last, mobile 'phone central heating application research has concerned itself with design models of domestic temperature setting and control. The latter are effected at a distance by means of mobile 'phones, to assure house owner comfort on returning home.

HCI research of acquiring and validating knowledge is also reflected in the activities of HCI designers and researchers of applications. This is the case, whether they are applied psychologists, design scientists, cognitive engineers, ease of use/usability experts, human-centred design consultants, or user experience (UX) design practitioners. However, although espousing different approaches to, and frameworks for, research and producing different kinds of knowledge to support different kinds of design practice, they all have the same HCI general problem of design and the same HCI particular scope of humans interacting with computers to do something as desired.

1.2.3.2 STATE OF HCI RESEARCH

HCI research acquires and validates knowledge to support HCI practices in solving the general HCI problem of design with the particular scope of humans interacting with computers to do something as desired. The state comprises knowledge and practices, which are exemplified as follows.

Concerning HCI knowledge, Internet banking research has developed standards, which address customers' requirements for paying bills, for transferring money and for recording their savings. Multi-media research has concerned itself with producing theories, reflecting the sharing of communications and images among colleagues and customers. Last, central heating research has concerned itself with heuristics for relating domestic temperatures to user comfort, contingent on outside temperatures and homeowner preferences.

As concerns HCI practices of research and design, these can be characterised as interdisciplinary overlapping fields (Rogers, 2012). The latter comprise—human factors, cognitive engineering, HCI, cognitive ergonomics, computer-supported cooperative work (CSCW), and information systems. Together they have developed practices of trial and error, implement and test, implement test and evaluate for the applications cited earlier, involving the acquisition and validation of HCI knowledge.

For a more detailed exemplification of the HCI particular scope, consider the two case studies, summarised in Chapter 9.

The domestic energy planning and control case study (see § 9.1 and Figure 1.1) has the general problem of the design of energy planning and control interactive systems, comprising the specification and implementation of such systems. The latter have the particular scope of home occupiers, interacting with computers for the planning and controlling of their comfort preference, as desired. The case study is itself an example of HCI research in that it reports the acquisition of initial HCI-EDPs for the domain of domestic energy planning and control.

The business-to-consumer electronic commerce case study (see § 9.2 and Figure 1.1) has the general problem of the design of the business-to-consumer electronic commerce interactive systems, comprising the specification and implementation of such systems. The latter have the particular scope of buyers, interacting with computers for the purchase of physical goods, such as tea and information goods, such as alarm alerts, as desired. The case study is itself an example of HCI research in that it reports the acquisition of initial HCI-EDPs for the domain of business-to-consumer electronic commerce.

REVIEW

HCI either comprises, or is associated with, many different types of discipline with different values and criteria, as identified earlier. However, for the purpose of acquiring initial HCI-EDPs, the HCI discipline is assumed to comprise—the HCI general problem of design with the particular scope of users interacting with computers to do something as desired. Also included is HCI research, as the acquisition and validation of knowledge to support practices in solving the general HCI problem. This conception forms the basis for the following chapter on HCI design.

1.3   PRACTICE ASSIGNMENT

Describe the assumptions made by what you understand by the term HCI general problem (as described in § 1.2.1), HCI particular scope (as described in § 1.2.2), and HCI research (as described in § 1.2.3). If you have no clear understanding of the HCI general problem/particular scope/research, as described, of your own at this time, select the expressions offered by your supervisor/instructor/teacher. Alternatively, select expressions from a suitable publication from the HCI research literature, which is different from the ones proposed here. Readers may, of course, do both.

- Contrast the similarities and differences between the assumptions made by your (or other's) understanding and those made here. Summarise the similarities and differences in the manner of Figure 1.1.

- How might the differences be made coherent?

- If they cannot be made coherent, why might this be so?

Hints and Tips

Difficult to get started?

Try reading the chapter again, while at the same time thinking about how to describe your own understanding (or that of others). Note similarities and differences between the two lines of thought, as you go along.

- Describe your understanding (or that of others) in its own terms, before attempting to apply those proposed here.

Difficult to complete?

Familiarise yourself with the main ways of understanding HCI, identified in the HCI research literature, before attempting to address those proposed here.

Test

List from memory as many of the section titles as you can.

CHAPTER 2

HCI Design

SUMMARY

The chapter introduces design, then HCI design. The latter comprises the HCI practices of specification and implementation of interactive human-computer systems, as desired. These HCI practices apply HCI design knowledge, acquired by HCI research, to support HCI design. The latter is conceived as the general problem of the HCI discipline for the purpose of acquiring initial HCI-EDPs. The latter are summarised in Chapter 9 and reported fully in the companion volume (Long et al., 2022, in press). Other discipline conceptions are referenced in contrast. The introduction, together with the previous chapter, form the basis for the following chapter on HCI knowledge.

2.1 DESIGN

Specification and implementation constitute a high-level categorisation of design practice. For example, engineering specifies and implements engineering artefacts. Specific engineering design, such as espoused by the sub-discipline of civil engineering, specifies and implements specific civil engineering artefacts such as bridges and buildings. Electronic engineering design specifies and implements circuits and control systems. Engineering design specifications are expressed in different ways. Bridges and buildings can be specified as drawings and maquettes, before implementation as simulations or initial structures. Circuits and control systems can be specified as digital images and models, before implementation as mock-ups or successive system versions.

Design further comprises practices and the knowledge, required to support them. Design practices include specify; specify and implement; implement and test; specify, implement, and iterate; and specify then implement. Design knowledge includes theories and principles. For example, column stress principles for buildings and electromagnetic principles for circuits.

2.2 HCI DESIGN

The HCI general problem, as assumed here for the acquisition of initial HCI-EDPs, is HCI design. The latter comprises specification and implementation (see also Long, 2021). The relationship is shown in Figure 2.1, which should be compared with Figures 1.1 and Figures 3–8.1 for similarities and differences. Likewise, as a format for alternative conceptions, which readers might like to formulate for themselves.

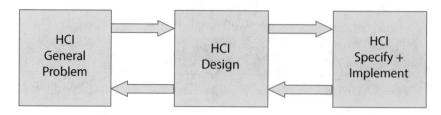

Figure 2.1: HCI general problem.

The conceptions of the HCI general problem may take different forms for different purposes and to embody different values. For example, in approaches and frameworks for HCI design there are differences in this respect between innovation, art, craft, engineering, applied, and science (Long, 2021). Further, according to Rogers (2012), there are six different HCI design practices—graphic design, product design, artist design, industrial design, and film design. Last, there are the so-called "movements," such as UX (user experience) design (Ritter, Baxter, and Churchill, 2014), agile design (Hartson and Pyla, 2018), and engagement design (Zagalo, 2020).

All these different approaches and frameworks, practice designs, and movements may have their own conceptions of HCI design, which may be appropriate for their own types of application. For example, design of UX interfaces for good games and banking application experiences. Also, design of interfaces for spreadsheet and personal communication applications using Agile methods. The latter involving animated sketch representations, before implementation as simulations. Games and banking applications can be designed for engagement using wire model representations, before implementation as simulations. HCI design practices include, among others, trial and error, and specify, implement, and test.

However, they are not the conception underlying the present quest for HCI-EDPs. The general HCI design specifies and implements HCI artefacts.[1] Specific HCI design, such as user interface design for interactive human-computer systems satisfying user and other requirements, specifies and implements specific artefacts.

A specific and more detailed exemplification of HCI design as specification and implementation follows. It is taken from the domestic energy planning and control case study, summarised in Chapter 9 (Stork, 1999) and reported in full in the companion volume to the present (Long et al., 2022, in press). It is not intended to illustrate specification and implementation in general. It certainly does not do that. However, it illustrates a set of user requirements, which has the potential of being re-expressed as a design problem, in which actual performance of the domestic heating system does not equal desired performance for the users. The expression is that of the HCI-specific scope of the general HCI design problem of a discipline of HCI, as required and applied for the acquisition of initial HCI-EDPs.

2.2.1   EXAMPLE OF USER REQUIREMENTS FOR HCI-EDPS

The user requirements for the design are:

> The domestic routine of X (house co-owner) occasionally requires them to remain at home to work in the mornings, rather than to leave earlier with his partner, Z (house co-owner), to work at the office. However, if X leaves after 8 a.m. or stays at home to work, then the house is too cold until they turn the gas-powered central heating back on. If they expect to be at home for a short time after 8 a.m., they often use the one-hour boost facility on the heating controller to turn the heating back on. This boost can result in them being too cold, if they are at home for longer than expected. X's ability to work is adversely affected by being cold and having to control the heating. X finds it difficult to plan much in advance, whether they are staying home to work or, if they stay, how long they will stay. The current gas bill is acceptable and an increase could be tolerated, although a decrease would be desirable.

2.2.2   EXAMPLE OF SPECIFICATION FOR HCI-EDPS

The artefact specification to satisfy these user requirements follows.

- "The existing controller does not have enough features to meet the user requirements. The specification of the new controller is:

  - To switch on in the morning at 6:40 a.m. and switch off at 10:00 p.m. during the week.

  - If the heating is turned off during a weekday, using an advance button, then the heating will turn on again in the early evening at 6:30 p.m.

  - To remain as the previous controller for the weekends.

  - To have an additional remote heating-controller, with an advance button and a bright status light, by the front door.

The occupants of the home need be instructed to use the heating controls as before, except that X should press the advance button on either controller, if the status light is "on" just before leaving to go to work during the week. X is to be considered the user of the designed artefact."

2.2.3   EXAMPLE OF IMPLEMENTATION FOR HCI-EDPS

The implementation, as a simulation, of the artefact specification, satisfying the user requirements follows.

- A controller in the same location as the existing one and an additional controller near the front door. (Rationale—to remind X to control the heating on leaving).
  - "The additional controller is implemented in the simulation simply to respond to the user's control commands. (Rationale—it is difficult, if not impossible, to allocate the user's leaving plan to the controller)."

2.3   CRITIQUE AND CHALLENGE FOR HCI DESIGN

HCI design has made much progress, since its inception. Both its scope and content continue to be developed and so to expand. Both HCI research and HCI practice reporting attest to this progress. However, the reliability of HCI design knowledge, such that the resulting HCI design specification results in desired performance, once implemented, has not generally been demonstrated. It cannot claim, then, to be known explicitly. Hence, the design practices of trial and error and implement and test.

This critique constitutes a challenge for HCI design and its associated knowledge. The latter needs to ensure that specifications of interactive human-computer systems, once implemented, result in desired performance without (or at least with fewer) trial-and-error iterations. However, this is not to dispute that specification per se has been shown to result in improved performance (Camara and Calvary, 2017).

Review

HCI design comprises the HCI practices of specification and implementation of interactive human-computer systems, as desired. These HCI practices apply HCI design knowledge, acquired by HCI research, to support HCI design. The latter is conceived as the general problem of the HCI discipline for the purpose of acquiring initial HCI-EDPs. Case studies of the latter are summarised in Chapter 9 and reported fully in the companion volume. Other design conceptions are referenced in contrast. The introduction, together with the previous chapter, form the basis for the following chapter on HCI knowledge.

2.4   PRACTICE ASSIGNMENT

2.4.1   GENERAL

Describe the assumptions made by what you understand by the term HCI design (see § 2.2), as specification and implementation. If you have no clear understanding of HCI design of your own at this time, select the expression offered by your supervisor/teacher/instructor. Alternatively, select an expression from a suitable publication from the HCI research literature.

- Contrast the similarities and differences between the assumptions made by your (or other's) understanding and those made here.

- How might the differences be made coherent?

- If they cannot be made coherent, why might this be so?

Hints and Tips

Difficult to get started?

Try reading the chapter again, while at the same time thinking about how to describe your own understanding (or that of others). Note similarities and differences between the two lines of thought, as you go along.

- Describe your understanding (or that of others) in its own terms, before attempting to apply those proposed here.

Difficult to complete?

Familiarise yourself with the main ways of understanding HCI design as specification and implementation, identified in the HCI research literature, before attempting to address those proposed here.

Test

List from memory as many of the section titles as you can.

2.4.2   PRACTICE SCENARIO

Practice Scenario 2.1: Create Your Own User, Requirements, Specification, and Implementation Example.

Select a domain, other than domestic energy planning and control, which interests you, with which you are familiar or which has been the subject of a report in the research literature.

- Create a set of possible user requirements, in the manner of § 2.2.1.

- Create an artefact specification to meet the user requirements, in the manner of § 2.2.2.

- Create an implementation as simulation, in the manner of § 2.2.3.

The example can only be very general and should be brief. The idea is to familiarise the reader with the concepts, as they relate to HCI design.

2.5   NOTES

[1] The concept of implementation here may be understood in two different senses.

> First, it is sometimes taken to mean the implementation of the specification of an interactive human-computer system, which, once tested, might then be followed by a new specification. Such iterations might continue, until some criterion is met. The latter may be in turn implemented and so on. This is the case, for example, for the HCI design practices of specify, implement, test and iterate.

> Second, implementation might be taken to mean the final version of an implemented specification before commercial manufacture or build.

The two notions of implementation might be associated with different practitioners. For example, HCI practitioners might be expected to use simulations to implement specifications as part of specify, implement, test, and iterate HCI design practice. In contrast, software engineering practitioners might be expected to implement the final commercial version of a specified interactive human-computer system in terms of computer software.

The difference constitutes an issue for the disciplines of HCI and software engineering, their researchers and their practitioners. However, it is not required to address the issue here. The first meaning is assumed in what follows and throughout the book. Any use of the second meaning is made clear on the occasion of its use.

CHAPTER 3

HCI Knowledge

SUMMARY

The chapter introduces knowledge, then HCI knowledge. The latter comprises declarative (or substantive) knowledge and procedural (or methodological) knowledge. Together, both types of knowledge constitute HCI design knowledge, acquired by HCI research to support HCI design practice in solving the HCI general problem of design. The conception is espoused for the purpose of acquiring initial HCI-EDPs, summarised in Chapter 9 and reported fully in the companion volume (Long et al., 2022, in press). Other discipline conceptions are referenced in contrast. The introduction, together with the previous two chapters, form the basis for the following chapter on HCI design knowledge.

3.1 KNOWLEDGE

Many different types of knowledge have been distinguished for different purposes and having different attributes and associated values. Here, knowledge is divided into two basic types: declarative (or substantive) and procedural (or methodological).1 Generally speaking, declarative knowledge expresses the "what" of design and knowledge expresses the "how" of design. Here, the terms "declarative" and "procedural" are used. However, the equivalence declarative/substantive and procedural/ methodological holds in all cases. For example, general engineering design practice is supported by declarative knowledge in the form of design models and procedural knowledge in the form of design methods. Specific engineering design practice, such as civil engineering, is supported by declarative knowledge in the form of bridge and building design models and procedural knowledge in the form of bridge and building model design methods. Likewise, electronic engineering design is supported by declarative knowledge in the form of circuit and control system models and procedural knowledge in the form of circuit and control system model design methods. Declarative and procedural knowledge support design practices of specification and implementation (see § 2.2).

3.2 HCI KNOWLEDGE

HCI knowledge, like knowledge more generally, can also be distinguished as two types: declarative HCI and procedural HCI (see also Long, 2021). The distinction is assumed here for the acquisition of initial HCI-EDPs. The relationship is shown in Figure 3.1, as it relates to HCI practice. The figure should be compared with Figures 1–2.1 and 4–8.1 for similarities and differences. Likewise, as a format for alternative conceptions, which readers might like to formulate for themselves.

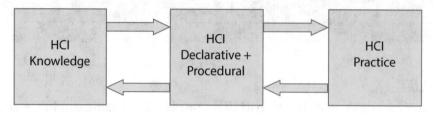

Figure 3.1: HCI knowledge.

Declarative HCI knowledge expresses the "what" of the HCI design of interactive human-computer systems and procedural knowledge expresses the "how" of the HCI design of such systems. For example, general HCI design practice is supported by declarative knowledge in the form of design models and procedural knowledge in the form of design methods. Specific HCI design practice, such as website design, is supported by declarative knowledge in the form of website design models and procedural knowledge in the form of website model design methods. Likewise, social media design is supported by declarative knowledge in the form of social media models and procedural knowledge in the form of social media model design methods. HCI knowledge supports HCI design practices of specification and implementation (see § 2.2). Exemplification and illustration of declarative design knowledge as models can be found in Hevner et al. (2004). Likewise, for procedural knowledge as methods in Hartson and Pyla (2018).

A specific and more detailed exemplification of HCI knowledge as declarative and procedural follows. It is taken from the business-to-consumer case study, summarised in Chapter 9 (Cummaford, 2007) and reported in full in the companion volume (Long et al., 2022, in press). It is not intended to illustrate declarative and procedural HCI knowledge in general nor per se. It proposes, and so illustrates, the detailed conceptualisation of users and computers as structures and behaviours, comprising the work system and which achieve a "product goal." In addition, how the latter is operationalised and relates to design problems and their solutions. The conception is that of HCI declarative and procedural design knowledge, as required and applied in the case study for the acquisition of initial HCI-EDPs.

3.2.1   EXAMPLE OF DECLARATIVE AND PROCEDURAL HCI KNOWLEDGE FOR HCI-EDPS

"Declarative HCI engineering design principles prescribe the features and properties of artefacts, which constitute a design solution to a design problem. Procedural HCI engineering design principles prescribe the methods for solving a design problem. The specification of declarative design knowledge and of the procedural design knowledge, operationalised during its acquisition, are required aspects of HCI-EDP development.

HCI-EDPs contain declarative and procedural design knowledge, which may be applied to any design problem within their scope. The declarative component is characterised by the conceptualisation of user and computer structures and behaviours, comprising the worksystem (sic), present in some instance of the class of users (U-class) or class of computers (C-class), respectively. The declarative component supports the conceptualisation of a task goal structure, comprising task goals, to be effected by the worksystem, which achieves the product goal stated in P-class. The product goal specifies the work to be effected in the domain by the worksystem, in terms of object attribute value transformations. The structures and behaviours of the declarative component are sufficient to achieve the task goal structure of the procedural component to an acceptable level of task quality (Tq), while incurring an acceptable level of costs to the user and to the computer, respectively (Uc, Cc). Task quality and worksystem costs are members of P-class. This sufficiency is supported by empirical testing of a class HCI-EDPs, which indicates its fitness-for-purpose.

A conception of HCI-EDPs, within which guarantees may be developed for associated design knowledge, is proposed. The conception comprises the following concepts and relationships.

For any design problem {user, computer, desired performance—Pd} and an HCI-EDP {U-class, C-class, P-class, declarative component, procedural component}:

1. If user is a member of U-class and computer is a member of C-class, then user structures and behaviours and computer structures and behaviours, as stated in the declarative component, are present.

2. If user structures and behaviours and computer structures and behaviours as specified by the declarative component are present, then the task goal structure specified by the procedural component is achievable.

3. If the task goal structure specified in the procedural component is effected by a worksystem comprising the structures and behaviours specified in the declarative component, then the product goal will be achieved, task quality will be x, user costs will be y, and computer costs will be z.

4. If task quality x, user costs y, and computer costs z are achieved, then actual performance (Pa) equals desired performance (Pd), that is, Pa = Pd.

5. Therefore, Pd is a member of P-class for a worksystem comprising instances of U-class and C-class.

Conception coherence derives from two relationships—that between the task goal structure and Tq for some product goal and that between the worksystem (sic) structures and behaviours, sufficient to achieve this task goal structure and Uc and Cc. These relationships are coherent, as performance is a function of the effectiveness with which some task goal structures are achieved by some worksystem structures and behaviours. The general HCI-EDP conception is complete, as it comprises the concepts of the engineering discipline of HCI, which inform its development. The issue of fitness-for-purpose is addressed by operationalisation of the conception of the general HCI-EDP. The latter informs the development of class HCI-EDPs, which may then be tested and generalised."

3.3   CRITIQUE AND CHALLENGE FOR HCI KNOWLEDGE

HCI knowledge has progressed since its inception. Both its scope and content continue to be expanded and so developed. HCI knowledge reporting and the burgeoning of applications attest to this progress (Ritter et al, 2014; Hartson and Pyla, 2018; Zagalo, 2020). However, the reliability of HCI knowledge, such that HCI design practice is supported with an assured outcome as desired, has not been convincingly demonstrated and so cannot claim to be known explicitly. Hence, the design practices of trial and error and implement and test.

This critique constitutes a challenge for HCI knowledge. The latter needs to ensure that its support for HCI practice as the design of interactive human-computer systems, as desired to satisfy user and other requirements, occurs without (or with fewer) trial-and-error iterations.

REVIEW

The chapter introduces knowledge and HCI knowledge for the purpose of acquiring HCI-EDPs. Knowledge is conceived as comprising two basic types: declarative knowledge and procedural knowledge. Both types of knowledge constitute HCI design knowledge, which supports HCI design practice. The reliability of this support is questioned by the critique. The introduction, together with the two previous chapters, forms the basis for the following chapter on HCI design knowledge.

3.4   PRACTICE ASSIGNMENT

3.4.1   GENERAL

Describe the assumptions made by your understanding of HCI knowledge (see § 3.2), as declarative and procedural. If you have no clear understanding of your own at this time, select the expression offered by your supervisor/instructor/teacher. Alternatively, select an expression from a suitable publication from the HCI research literature.

- Contrast the similarities and differences between the assumptions made by your (or other's) understanding and those made here.

- How might the differences be made coherent?

- If they cannot be made coherent, why might this be so?

Hints and Tips

Difficult to get started?

Try reading the chapter again, while at the same time thinking about how to describe your own understanding (or that of others). Note similarities and differences between the two lines of thought, as you go along.

- Describe your understanding (or that of others) in its own terms, before attempting to apply those proposed here.

Difficult to complete?

Familiarise yourself with the main ways of understanding HCI design as specification and implementation, identified in the HCI research literature, before attempting to address those proposed here.

Test

List from memory as many of the section titles as you can.

3.4.2   PRACTICE SCENARIO

Practice Scenario 3.1 Create Your Own Declarative and Procedural Example.

Select a domain, other than business-to-consumer electronic commerce, which interests you, with which you are familiar or which has been the subject of a report in the research literature.

- Create a set of possible declarative proposals, as described in § 3.2.

- Create a set of possible procedural proposals, as described in § 3.2.

The example can only be very general, but the idea is to familiarise the reader with the concepts, as they relate to HCI knowledge.

3.5   NOTES

[1] Contextual knowledge and somatic knowledge are also identified as basic types of knowledge, as well as declarative and procedural knowledge. However, although the concepts of context and soma have found some use in HCI, such use is far from general and it is not required by the classification of HCI design knowledge, required and applied for the acquisition of initial HCI-EDPs, as proposed here.

Further classifications of knowledge also exist. For example, knowledge can be explicit, as in documented information, implicit, as in applied information and tacit, as in understood information. The explicit/implicit distinction with respect to HCI design knowledge is used to distinguish types of such knowledge (see § 4.2). However, the distinction is not required by the classification of HCI design knowledge as offered here. The distinction, however, is required later to distinguish the types of HCI design knowledge.

CHAPTER 4

HCI Design Knowledge

SUMMARY

The chapter introduces design knowledge, then HCI design knowledge. The latter comprises the HCI practices of specification and implementation of interactive human-computer systems, as desired. Support is provided by declarative and procedural HCI design knowledge, acquired by HCI research. The discipline conception is espoused for the purpose of acquiring initial HCI-EDPs, summarised in Chapter 9 and reported fully in the companion volume (Long et al., 2022, in press). Other discipline conceptions are referenced in contrast. A critique of HCI design knowledge is offered in the form of its lack of known reliability. This lack constitutes a challenge for HCI design knowledge in general.

4.1   DESIGN KNOWLEDGE

Different types of design knowledge have been distinguished for different purposes and having different attributes and associated values. Here, design is taken to comprise specification and implementation (see § 2.1and § 2.5 Note 1). Knowledge is taken to comprise two basic types—declarative and procedural (see § 3.1 and § 3.5 Note 1). Design knowledge, then, supports declarative and procedural specification, which is then implemented. Together they inform, for example, the design of engineering artefacts. Specific engineering design knowledge, such as possessed by the sub-disciplines of civil engineering and electronic engineering, support declarative and procedural specification and its implementation in the form of models and methods. Such design knowledge is associated with specific artefact domains, such as bridges and buildings for civil engineering and circuits and control systems for electronic engineering. Design knowledge is central to such sub-disciplines of engineering and the associated research.

4.2   HCI DESIGN KNOWLEDGE

HCI design knowledge, like design knowledge more generally, can also be distinguished as two types—declarative and procedural specification, which is then implemented (see also Long, 2021). The distinction is assumed here for the acquisition of initial HCI-EDPs. Together they support the design of interactive human-computer systems to satisfy user and other requirements. The relationship is shown in Figure 4.1. The figure should be compared with Figures 1–3.1 for similarities and differences. Likewise, as a format for alternative conceptions, which readers might like to formulate for themselves.

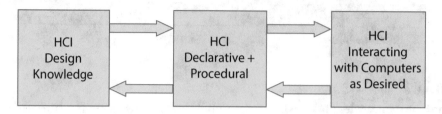

Figure 4.1: HCI design knowledge.

Specific HCI design knowledge supports declarative and procedural specification for their implementation to support HCI design practice with the scope of humans interacting with computers, as desired. HCI design knowledge has been applied in the domains of air traffic management and logistics planning and control, in the form of wire-frame models and structured analysis and design methods. Wire-frame models express the "what" of HCI design knowledge, that is, interactive human-computer systems. Agile methods express the "how" of HCI design knowledge, that is, how to design interactive human-computer systems. HCI design knowledge has also been applied in the domains of Internet banking and social media in the form of persona models and craft design methods. Examples of different types of HCI design knowledge are described and exemplified later in the book, including craft artefacts and design practice experience (see § 5.1), models and methods (see § 6.1), and principles, rules, and heuristics (see § 7.1). Further exemplification and illustration of design knowledge as models can be found in Hevner et al. (2004). Likewise, as methods in Hartson and Pyla (2018).

A specific and more detailed exemplification of HCI design knowledge follows. The latter is used to support HCI design practice with the particular scope of humans interacting with computers to do something as desired. The examples are taken from the two case studies, summarised in Chapter 9 (Stork, 1999 and Cummaford, 2007) and reported in full in the companion volume (Long et al., 2022, in press). It is not intended to illustrate HCI design knowledge in general nor per se. Nor is it intended to illustrate the specific HCI MUSE design method nor the HCI design guidelines used. The illustration is that of HCI design knowledge, as required and applied in the case studies for the acquisition of initial HCI-EDPs.

4.2.1   EXAMPLE OF GUIDELINES APPLIED TO DOMESTIC ENERGY PLANNING AND CONTROL FOR ACQUIRING HCI-EDPS

The example from the domain of domestic energy planning and control (also used to exemplify HCI design in § 2.2) is taken from the Design Synthesis Phase of MUSE (Method for USability

Engineering, Lim and Long, 1994). The extract describes the application of HCI design knowledge in the form well-known guidelines (declarative design knowledge) and of a structured analysis and design method (procedural design knowledge—see § 4.2). The MUSE phases and products follow. The guidelines example follows.

- "A text summary of the interaction concerns is constructed (Statement of User Needs), based on the user requirements and the analysis of the existing system. The statement contains:
    ○ Explicit design criteria, such as the need for the artefact cost to be acceptable for the benefits.

    ○ Implicit design criteria, such as the retention of the existing functionality of the controller to support non-weekday-morning tasks.

    ○ Explicit system performance criteria, such as X must not be cold.

- Implicit performance criteria, such as X (a house co-owner), must be permitted to leave home, when they desire (constraining should not be considered suitable for the artefact specification).

    ○ Relevant design knowledge, such as an extension of a guideline by Shneiderman (1983) that "human action should be eliminated where no [human] judgement is required" to include "and minimise human action where human judgement is required." This extended guideline confirms the essential task-level decision expressed earlier.

The conceptual design of the conjoint user and computer tasks is advanced (Composite Task Model), maintaining consistency with the accepted foundation of the task-level design developed in the previous phase. Important design decisions are now rationalised—a controller in the same location as the existing one and another controller near the front door.

The design is considered at a lower level of detail by the decomposition of the on-line tasks (System Task Model). At this stage, the guidelines of "transfer of learning," "feedback," and "consistency" (Smith and Mosier, 1986) are applied. For example, transfer of learning is supported by porting effective existing tasks to the target system.

Allocation of function between the user and the artefact is considered. It is difficult, if not impossible, to allocate the user's leaving plan to the controller. So, the controller simply responds to the user's control commands. This allocation corresponds with the HCI guideline that humans are generally better than computers at "drawing on experience and adapting decisions to situations" (Shneiderman, 2010). The additional remote heating-controller is justified as reminding X to control the heating on leaving.

There is no reporting of whether or not the HCI design knowledge had the effect claimed for it. In other words, whether or not the guidelines were reliable. This issue is addressed in § 4.3 and elsewhere in the book. It constitutes the challenge faced by HCI design knowledge. For the purposes in hand, however, it is sufficient to identify the HCI design knowledge, which the designer intended and attempted to apply to exemplify the latter's application to design, as part of the case study to acquire initial HCI-EDPs.

4.2.2   EXAMPLE OF GUIDELINES APPLIED TO BUSINESS-TO-CONSUMER ELECTRONIC COMMERCE FOR ACQUIRING HCI-EDPS

The example from the domain of business-to-consumer electronic commerce (also used to exemplify HCI knowledge in § 3.2) is taken from a listing of HCI e-commerce design guidelines, used to design screens, that is, to specify them and to implement them in the form of a simulation, used for testing. The guidelines example follows.

> "The computer structures sufficient to support the participant and computer behaviours in the task goal structure were then identified, and grouped into screens. Existing declarative knowledge from HCI and design literature was then applied during the specification of each screen. For example, the following guidelines characterise the kind of knowledge, which is typically expressed as recommendations for design features to include or avoid:

1. All sites should use the same standard label for the "shopping cart."

2. Don't force participants to register their personal details with the site before allowing them to add products to their basket.

3. Use the label "add to basket" rather than "buy" to get customers to add a product to their basket ("buy" mistakenly suggests final commitment by the customer).

4. Provide a link to the shopping basket on every page.

5. Include links from products in the shopping basket back to their product description pages.

6. Avoid making additional offers to the customer as they are trying to add a product to the basket.

7. Provide feedback to the customer confirming that an item has been added to their basket.

8. Allow customers to remove items from their basket easily.

9. Let customers return to where they were shopping previously from the shopping basket page.

10. Save the contents of abandoned shopping carts for the customer to use in future visits.

11. Ensure that customers always know how many steps there are in the checkout process and where they are within that process.

12. Ensure that customers are told the total cost of their purchase (including delivery) before requiring them to register."

Similar guidelines, specific to the domain of e-commerce transaction systems, are also applied, as listed by other authors (Bidigare, 2000; Chaparro, 2001; Kienan, 2001; Walsh, 2003). These were reviewed and applied during specification of the task goal structure screens.

Terminology used for labelling of computer physical structures (for example, buttons used to add items to the participant's order) was also informed by a report involving 100 leading UK e-shops, carried out by Snow Valley (2005a). The latter notes, for example, that a button with the text "add to basket" was the most prevalent form of control for adding an item to the customer's order, in the shops surveyed. However, relevance does not necessarily imply that these design features are in any way optimal, or more effective than alternative design features. Nielsen (1993) claims that participants spend most of their time on other websites. Thus, adopting popular design conventions increases participant comprehension through familiarity. Hence, it was considered to be apposite for the domain of e-commerce. The positioning of physical structures on each screen was informed by studies of participants' expectations about the relative positioning of the controls (Bernard, 2002; Bernard and Sheshandri, 2004). For example, participants might expect the "go to your shopping basket" control to be positioned in the top right area of every screen, other than the checkout screens and shopping basket screen itself.

A second report by Snow Valley (2005b) surveyed the most common incidence and ordering of payment input fields on 100 UK e-shops. There was a wide variation, with little consensus on the number or type of fields required (for example, the most common set of controls was card type, number, "cv2 number," a three-digit code found on the signature strip of a credit card, used for card authentication during online purchasing), issue, start and expiry, used by only 3 of the 100 e-shops surveyed). The class design payment screen grouped the fields with mandatory entry together at the top (that is, name, card type, number, expiry date, security code), followed by the Switch issue number and start date input boxes, which were only mandatory for cards, which featured this information.

In the Snow Valley report (2005b), the cv2 number was referred to using 27 different terms, by the 82 who requested it, out of the 100 e-shops surveyed. The most popular term used by 27 of the e-shops was "security code," and so this was used in the class design solution payment screen.

There is no reporting of whether or not the HCI design knowledge had the effect claimed for it. This issue is address in § 4.3 and elsewhere in the book. For the purposes in hand, however, it is sufficient to identify the HCI design knowledge, which the designer intended and attempted to apply to exemplify the latter's application to design to illustrate the latter's application to design, as part of the case study to acquire initial HCI-EDPs.

4.3   CRITIQUE AND CHALLENGE FOR HCI DESIGN KNOWLEDGE

HCI design knowledge continues to grow. Both its scope and content continue to evolve. HCI knowledge reporting and the great number of new applications attest to these developments and associated movements (Ritter et al, 2014; Hartson and Pyla, 2018; Zagalo, 2020). However, the effectiveness of HCI design knowledge, such that HCI design practices are supported with an acceptable reliability, has not been persuasively demonstrated and so cannot be claimed as known explicitly. Hence, the continued adoption by designers of the practices of trial and error and implement and test.

This critique constitutes a challenge for HCI design knowledge. The latter needs better to ensure that its support for HCI practice as the design of interactive human-computer systems to satisfy user and other requirements occurs with less trial-and-error iterations. Later chapters suggest how different types of HCI design knowledge, including craft artefacts and design practice experience, models and methods, and principles, rules, and heuristics design knowledge might meet this challenge.

REVIEW

The chapter introduces design knowledge and HCI design knowledge for the purpose of acquiring HCI-EDPs. The latter comprise declarative knowledge, for example, in the form of models and procedural knowledge, for example, in the form of methods. Both models and methods support the specification and implementation of interactive human-computer systems to satisfy user and other requirements. HCI design knowledge, in the form of models and methods, support HCI design practice. The reliability of this support, however, is questioned. The introduction, together with the earlier chapters, forms the basis for the following chapters on types of HCI design knowledge, their critique, and the associated challenge.

4.4   PRACTICE ASSIGNMENT

Describe the assumptions made by your understanding of HCI design knowledge, as expressed in the form of declarative HCI design models and procedural HCI design methods for the purpose of the specification and implementation of interactive human-computer systems (see § 4.2). If you have no clear understanding of your own at this time, select the expression offered by your supervisor/instructor/teacher. Alternatively, select an expression from a suitable publication from the HCI research literature.

- Contrast the similarities and differences between the assumptions made by your (or other's) understanding and those made here.

- How might the differences be made coherent?

- If they cannot be made coherent, why might this be so?

Hints and Tips

Difficult to get started?

Try reading the chapter again, while at the same time thinking about how to describe your own understanding (or that of others). Note similarities and differences between the two lines of thought, as you go along.

- Describe your understanding (or that of others) in its own terms, before attempting to apply those proposed here.

Difficult to complete?

Familiarise yourself with the main ways of understanding HCI design knowledge, as expressed in the form of declarative HCI design models and procedural HCI design methods for the specification and implementation of interactive computer systems, identified in the HCI research literature, before attempting to address those proposed here.

Test

List from memory as many of the section titles as you can.

PART II

HCI Design Knowledge for HCI Engineering Design Principles

The second part of the book presents HCI design knowledge in general. Some HCI design knowledge is used in the HCI-EDP case studies. Other HCI design knowledge is to be contrasted with that of initial HCI-EDPs. The latter, as best-practice, could be used in future case studies of HCI-EDP acquisition. The design knowledge comprises craft artefacts and design practice experience, models and methods, and principles, rules, and heuristics. A critique and a challenge for each type of HCI design knowledge concern the reliability of the knowledge to support HCI design practice.

CHAPTER 5

HCI Design Knowledge as Craft Artefacts and Design Practice Experience

SUMMARY

The chapter introduces craft artefacts and design practice experience as HCI design knowledge. The latter is exemplified in the form of "best-practice" in supporting design directly but implicitly. Some examples are taken from the two case studies of HCI-EDP acquisition, summarised in Chapter 9 and reported in full in the companion volume (Long et al., 2022, in press). Other examples are presented in contrast. All examples, as best-practice, could be used to acquire future HCI-EDPs. Also presented is a critique of HCI design knowledge, its current state, and the associated challenge. Craft artefacts and design practice experience constitutes one form of HCI design knowledge. It is acquired and validated implicitly by HCI artefacts and design practice experience, to solve the general HCI problem of design with the particular scope of humans interacting with computers to do something as desired, as viewed from a discipline perspective. The introduction, as one type of HCI design knowledge, is followed in subsequent chapters by models and methods and principles, rule, and heuristics, as other types of HCI design knowledge.

5.1 CRAFT ARTEFACTS AND DESIGN PRACTICE EXPERIENCE HCI DESIGN KNOWLEDGE

HCI design knowledge, as craft artefacts and design practice experience, viewed from a discipline perspective, would assume HCI to be a discipline (see § 1.2) with a general problem (see § 1.2.1), a particular scope (see § 1.2.2) and which conducts HCI research (see § 2.3) (see also Long, 2021). These assumptions, however, are only implicit, unless claimed otherwise and explicitly. Many alternative assumptions, then, are also possible (see Camara and Calvary, 2017). At this time, craft artefacts and design practice experience constitutes the most pervasive form of design knowledge, acquired and validated by HCI research, to support, directly but implicitly, the practice of the design of humans interacting with computers to do something as desired. Again, all these assumptions are implicit and so alternative assumptions are possible (see Kim, 2020). HCI artefacts are an implicit expression of the declarative or "what" of HCI design, that is, the product of application design.

HCI design practice experience is an implicit expression of the procedural or "how" of HCI design, that is, the process of application design (see Zagalo, 2020). The relationship is shown in Figure 5.1, which should be compared with Figures 1–4.1 for similarities and differences. Likewise, as a format for alternative conceptions, which readers might like to formulate for themselves.

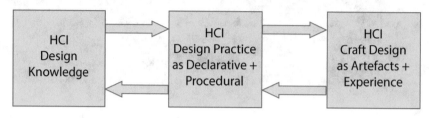

Figure 5.1: HCI design knowledge as craft artefact and design practice experience.

Craft artefacts and design practice experience have been involved in novel forms of HCI. For example, the innovation of the graphical user interface (GUI) resulted from a range of different artefacts and practices. The latter originating from Xerox, Apple, and other research and development organisations. The GUI was also the result of many different ideas and the experience afforded by the exchange of designers between such companies. Apple engineers worked in the Xerox Parc facilities. Parc employees subsequently moved to Apple to work on the Lisa and the Macintosh. Expert advice, design experience, and the design of other innovations supported both preliminary and final artefact versions.

Other innovative technologies, involving craft artefacts and practice design knowledge, include—multi-media, smell and taste, avatars, voice recognition, interactive robots, face recognition, dog tracking, and interactive group gaming.

These interactive technologies have been used by craft artefacts and practice design experience to implement and test interactive games, art, health, education, and communications applications.

5.2   STATE OF CRAFT ARTEFACTS AND DESIGN PRACTICE EXPERIENCE HCI DESIGN KNOWLEDGE

Craft design experience, as HCI design knowledge is implicit in artefacts. It can only be instanced by artefacts themselves, unless otherwise rendered explicit. Such artefacts include those associated with the novel interactive human-computer technologies, cited earlier. The latter include applications, such as, competitive team gaming, preliminary portrait sketching for later painting, real-time fitness monitoring, language acquisition progress, and air-to-land multi-media communications.

Attempts have been made to render craft artefact design knowledge explicit. Perhaps the best known and most successful attempt is reported by Carroll (2003 and 2010). He proposes "design rationale," as a theory, which supports the detailed description of the history and meaning of an artefact in the form of claims. The interpretation is then synthesised as the knowledge implicit in the designs. The latter can then be applied explicitly in subsequent designs. Only by rendering the artefact design features explicit in this way can the claims be conceptualised, operationalised, tested and generalised explicitly. The latter are as required by HCI research from a discipline perspective.

Craft practice HCI design knowledge is implicit in the experience of the designer. The experience is acquired by learning from other designers, by design teachers, by attending design workshops, by working alongside more experienced designers. Also, thinking up new designs and implementing them. Craft practice can be characterised as "trial and error" and "implement and test" and iterations of the same process. Craft design practice is implicit in the examples of artefacts described earlier.

As an example of craft artefacts and design practice experience, Balaam et al. (2015) note that breastfeeding is positively encouraged in many countries as a matter of public health. The World Health Organisation (WHO) recommends breastfeeding exclusively for the first six months of an infant's life. However, it may be difficult for women to meet this criterion for reasons of feeding technique and of social acceptance.

Balaam et al. report a "design and research" project, which specifies and implements an application called FeedFinder, a location-mapping mobile interactive service for breastfeeding women. However, the research status of the project is not entirely clear. It claims neither to acquire nor to validate HCI design knowledge explicitly. It does not count, then, as research from a discipline perspective, according to the definition presented in § 1.2.3.2. In contrast, its status as a design project is clear. It could be considered an example of design research, although the authors do not make such a claim. It also might be considered an example of best-practice. Again, the authors make no such claim.

The design of the FeedFinder application has four phases. These comprise—sensitising user-engagement, applying user-centred design, developing/deploying an application, and evaluation. In addition, Balaam et al. discuss how mobile technologies can be designed to achieve public health goals more generally. They suggest that related technologies may be better aimed at communities and societies, rather than at individuals, as currently. This, suggestion, however, amounts to an interesting speculation, which may, of course, be taken up by other researchers.

On what grounds might the Balaam et al. project be classified as a craft artefacts and design practice experience approach to HCI design? Such an approach requires the application of best-practice to designing human-computer interactions to satisfy user and other requirements in the form of an interactive system. Balaam et al. apply best-practice to the design of FeedFinder. The best-practice comprises user-engagement sensitisation, user-centred design techniques, application development, and deployment and evaluation of the extent to which the application meets the user and other requirements. These design practices, in conjunction with Balaam et al.'s own past and present design experience, along with ideas from current mobile artefact technology, constitute the best-practice.

In conclusion, Balaam et al.'s project is considered to exemplify a craft artefacts and design practice experience approach to HCI practice. It applies best-practice generic user-centred techniques. The acquisition or validation of new design knowledge, however, is not declared an explicit aim of the project. The best practice, as well as being in part generic, also derives from the researcher/designers' previous craft artefact design experience. The latter, enhanced by the FeedFinder design experience, would be expected to contribute to future such practice. The project report might also inform the practice of its readers, but this is not explicitly claimed or known.

A further example of craft artefacts and design practice experience is to be found in the domestic energy planning and control case study, summarised in Chapter 9. The example reflects the designer's craft artefact experience in the use of, and the associated reasoning about, the artefact, constituting the current central heating controller. For example, "the remote heating-controller is designed with an advance push button to ensure 'consistency' between the two controllers. Substantial porting of the existing design is possible, particularly with the layout of the two heating-controllers." It also reflects the craft artefact design decisions and associated design reasoning, concerning assessment of the panel of evaluators. "Although some initial objections are raised, after discussion none of these are considered relevant in terms of the artefact satisfying the user requirements. For example, some of the objections either asserted the artefact fulfilled more than the user requirements (but not less) or that the artefact might have embodied alternative design features." The MUSE method here is merely a carrier for this reporting as is the inclusion of the guidelines applied. The former is exemplified per se in Chapter 6 and the latter in Chapter 7.

The user requirements for the re-design of a home central heating system are elicited. Best-practice interactive system development then applies a structured analysis and design method (MUSE—Method for USability Engineering, Lim and Long, 1994) to the redesign of the homeowner's central heating system to satisfy their user requirements, as re-expressed in the form of a design problem. A summary of the best-practice follows. The researcher was a practising HCI software designer at the time.

"The current existing system is analysed in detail. Other existing systems are listed, but not analysed. A satisfactory artefact specification results from the first MUSE iteration. Two Task Descriptions are produced. First, a task analysis is conducted, based on an interview in which X (home co-owner with Z) introspects about their days (Task Description). Second, X is asked to keep a diary for several mornings, during which they stayed at home and left for work.

These Task Descriptions are generalised (Generalised Task Model of the existing system) to gain an understanding of "generic" mornings (which the design needs to support). The tables for the products for the existing system detail valuable observations, design implications, and speculations that arise. For example, it is observed that X appears to plan using an electronic diary and to-do list. The possibility of interfacing these with the heating control is considered, but dismissed. There is poor correspondence between the departure plan and the electronic diary and to-do list.

The final step develops a task-level conceptual design of the target system (General Task Model) based on the user requirements and the design implications and speculations, derived from the existing system. The task-level conceptual design documents the design decision to control the heating on departure.

The initial task-level conceptual design suggests a potential for re-use of more detailed existing system features. It was decided to perform a more detailed analysis of the existing system to support that potential. Accordingly, a range of MUSE products are developed that analyse the existing system from its conceptual to its detailed design For example, the Domain of Design Discourse of the existing system and its System Task Model. Analysis during the Information Elicitation and Analysis Phase is the basis of the design in the other phases.

The MUSE Design Synthesis Phase follows. A text summary of the interaction concerns is constructed (Statement of User Needs), based on the user requirements and the analysis of the existing system. The statement contains:

- explicit design criteria, such as the need for the artefact cost to be acceptable for the benefits;

- implicit design criteria, such as the retention of the existing functionality of the controller to support non-weekday-morning tasks;

- explicit system performance criteria, such as X must not be cold;

- implicit performance criteria, such as X must be permitted to leave home, when they desire (constraining should not be considered suitable for the artefact specification);

- relevant design knowledge, such as an extension of a guideline by Shneiderman (1983) that "human action should be eliminated where no [human] judgement is required" to include "and minimise human action where human judgement is required." This extended guideline confirms the essential task-level decision expressed earlier.

The conceptual design of the conjoint user and computer tasks is advanced (Composite Task Model), maintaining consistency with the accepted foundation of the task-level design developed in the previous phase. Important design decisions are now rationalised—a controller in the same location as the existing one and another controller near the front door.

The design is considered at a lower level of detail by the decomposition of the on-line tasks (System Task Model). At this stage, the guidelines of "transfer of learning," "feedback," and "consistency" are applied. For example, transfer of learning is supported by porting effective existing tasks to the target system.

Allocation of function between the user and the artefact is considered. It is difficult, if not impossible, to allocate the user's leaving plan to the controller. So, the controller simply responds to the user's control commands. This allocation corresponds with the HCI guideline that humans are generally better than computers at "drawing on experience and adapting decisions to situations."

The additional remote heating-controller is justified as reminding X to control the heating on leaving.

The third and final MUSE phase, that of Design Specification, follows. The interaction-level design is advanced (Interaction Task Model and Interface Model). The remote heating-controller is designed with an advance push button to ensure "consistency" between the two controllers. Substantial porting of the existing design is possible, particularly with the layout of the two heating-controllers (Pictorial Screen Layouts).

By way of evaluation, three informal analytic assessments of whether the artefact fulfils the user requirements are conducted, apart from the assessment of consistency through the application of MUSE. First, an analytic argument is constructed to show that the introduction of the artefact into the home of X and Z should "satisfy" the problem. A form of this analytic argument, commensurate with the user requirements, follows.

> "*The proposed artefact should support the domestic routine of X, which occasionally requires them to remain at home to work in the mornings, rather than leave earlier with their partner Z, to work at the office. If X leaves after 8a.m. or stays at home to work, then the house should remain warm without intervention. The design ensures that the gas-powered central heating remains on rather than turning itself off, which causes X to be uncomfortable, because the house cools. Since the house is no longer too cold, X is not required to turn the heating back on. Therefore, even if X expects to be at home for a short time after 8a.m. they should not need to use the one-hour boost facility for warmth. X's ability to work should no longer be adversely affected by being cold and having to control the heating. The house is now warm and the heating does not need controlling, until they finish working. X finds it difficult to plan in advance, whether they are staying at work and, if staying, for how long. The artefact should support this planning difficulty, as the heating should only need controlling to match the time of planning. The gas bill may increase by a small amount, which X and Z consider acceptable. X should not be overly taxed by turning the heating off, when leaving, or learning to turn the heating off. The cost of the artefact should be low (approximately £40 for a fully functioning prototype version).*"

The second informal analytic assessment involves a panel of nine practitioners, five human factors engineers and four software engineers, appraising the artefact specification produced using MUSE. They are all familiar with the method and the user requirements. Although some initial objections are raised, after discussion none of these are considered relevant in terms of the artefact satisfying the user requirements. For example, some of the objections either asserted the artefact fulfilled more than the user requirements (but not less) or that the artefact might have embodied alternative design features.

The third, and last, informal analytic assessment is an expert walkthrough of the artefact specification performed by a human factors engineer. Their report contains the following concluding statement:

> *"The likely behaviour of the occupants of the house as concerns the system is estimated with respect to a number of scenarios concerning different types of morning events. It is considered that in the scenario, where there was previously a problem (that is, when X remains at home after 8 a.m.), the system would solve the problem by maintaining X's comfort, and that X would remember to switch the system off, as long as the front door controller is located in a suitably prominent position. When X leaves the house early, their expectations of the system, based on the existing one, may initially cause them to forget to switch the heating off. They are currently not required to take any action, when leaving early in the morning. However, X would soon learn to adapt their morning routine to include the new task of switching the heating off. Similarly, if X left the house earlier than Z, they might forget to switch the heating off, as the normal morning routine does not require any action on Z's part. However, if the system status is designed to be conspicuous, and the controller is prominently located, these problems would be less likely to occur, than if the controller were located in a less visible position. At present, there is no evidence in the user requirements or in the analysis of the existing systems that X will ever leave earlier than Z. Further consultation with X confirms this and so the problem of Z having to remember to operate the system would occur very (and acceptably) infrequently."*

In addition, an empirical assessment is performed by constructing a faithful prototype (which does not alter the state of the heating) of the remote heating controller and re-programming the existing controller. This prototype is placed by the front door and the occupants given instruction on its use. This assessment confirms the analytic argument. No empirical assessment of the gas bill increase is conducted.

Taken together, the analytic and empirical assessments demonstrate informally that the artefact specification fulfils the user requirements.

A further example of craft artefacts and design practice experience is to be found in the business-to-consumer electronic commerce case study, summarised in Chapter 9.

The example comprises the specific design solution to a specific design problem, identified on a live information goods electronic commerce website. The researcher, who was also the designer and a practising HCI designer at the time, used best -practice to develop new screens, which contributed to solving the design problem.

The homepage of the specific design solution for information goods (see Figure 5.2) differs from that of the specific design problem homepage. The prices of single items and subscriptions are clearly displayed, and the login boxes for existing users to manage their subscriptions are clearly shown. Thus, the designer applies their craft artefacts and design experience to features of the problem artefact to inform the features of the solution artefact.

In addition, the sign-up page presents single purchase and subscription options, with pricing for each. This ensures that the user is informed of the costs prior to purchase. The latter design judgement derives from the prior craft artefact experience of the designer.

The user's selected package and its price are then displayed on both the validation code entry screen and the confirmation screen. For the Enter Details Page (Single Purchase) see Figure 5.3.

Figure 5.2: Specific design solution—homepage.

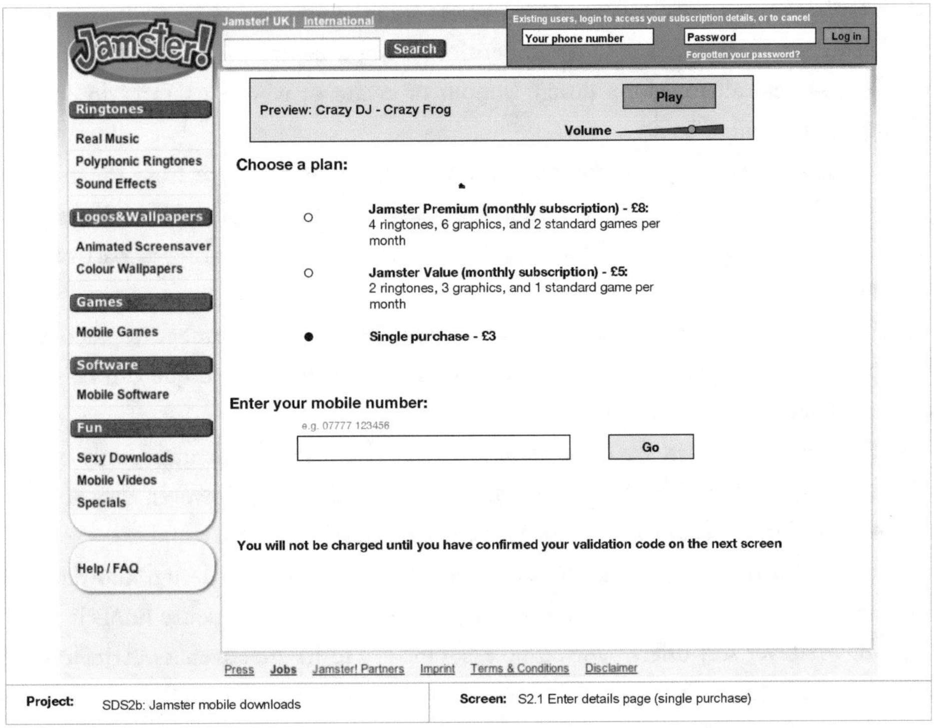

Figure 5.3: Enter details page (single purchase).

5.3   CRITIQUE AND CHALLENGE FOR CRAFT ARTEFACTS AND DESIGN PRACTICE EXPERIENCE AS HCI DESIGN KNOWLEDGE

To be validated, craft artefacts and practice HCI design knowledge needs to be conceptualised, operationalised, tested, and generalised, as viewed from a discipline perspective (see § 1.2.3.1–2). However, the design knowledge is implicit in the artefact itself and in the designer's experience. Such validation, then, can be assessed only indirectly and implicitly. Such validation, however, is extensive. It takes many forms and is to be found over a wide range of people and organisations. Such validation, however, is rarely made explicit as such and organised in such a way, as to support designer consensus and agreed progress. Alternative criteria may, of course, be applied, for example, as in the case of design research (see Roedl and Stolterman, 2013).

A critique by the designers themselves of an artefact can be expressed by the number of "implement and test" iterations required for another interactive-system version, especially if they consider the number to be excessive for some reason. A critique by other designers is expressed when they criticise a designer colleague and assess their reputation as being inexpert. Also, if a designer fails to win a prize in a design competition, is not accepted as a member of a professional design body, is not nominated for a design honour or award or whose artefacts do not appear on "best selling/most popular" lists.[1]

A critique can also be presumed on the basis of negative feedback from the users of interactive human-computer systems. Such feedback is sought by the suppliers of such systems. It can either be given on-line, by means of user panels or result from user testing as part of the system development process.

A critique can also be presumed from artefact producers, if the number of practice iterations for a new product, delays its release date. Last, an artefact acquirer's critique can be expressed in cancelled orders and a change of supplier.

Such critiques, however, are to be found in the HCI research literature, only by exception, although more may be found in the professional designer literature. However, they are implicit in the behaviours of designers, users and interactive system developers and suppliers.

Craft artefacts and design practice experience, as a form of HCI design knowledge, is to be judged by the effectiveness of its support for HCI design. Simply to espouse implicit HCI design knowledge of whatever sort offers by itself no assurance as to its effectiveness. Artefacts and practice alone are unable to provide such assurance. The challenge, then, for HCI design knowledge in general, including for HCI artefacts and design practice experience in particular, is how to ensure the effectiveness of the implicit knowledge, which they offer in support of HCI design.

Review

The chapter characterises craft artefacts and design practice experience as implicit HCI design knowledge, supporting design directly. It also describes and critiques their current state and identifies the associated challenge. Craft artefacts and design practice experience constitute a form of HCI design knowledge. The latter is acquired and validated implicitly by HCI artefacts and practice, to solve the general HCI problem of design with the particular scope of humans interacting with computers to do something as desired, as viewed from a discipline perspective. The latter is espoused here for the development of HCI-EDPs. The introduction, as a type of HCI design knowledge, is followed in subsequent chapters by other types of design knowledge in the form of models and methods and principles, rules and heuristics.

5.4   PRACTICE ASSIGNMENT

Describe the assumptions made by your research as concerns—HCI artefacts, HCI design practice experience, and conjoint HCI artefacts and practice, as HCI design knowledge to support HCI design (see § 5.1 and § 5.2). If you have no research of your own at this time, select suitable research of a colleague or supervisor/teacher/instructor. Alternatively, select a suitable publication either from the HCI research literature or from the HCI design professional literature.

- Contrast the similarities and differences between the assumptions made by your (or that of other's) research and the proposals made here.

- How might the differences be made coherent?

- If they cannot be made coherent, why might this be so?

Hints and Tips

Difficult to get started?

Try reading the chapter again, while at the same time thinking about how to describe your own (or that of others) HCI design artefacts and design practice experience, as HCI design knowledge. Note similarities and differences between the two lines of thought, as you go along.

- Describe your (or that of others) HCI craft artefacts and design practice experience, as HCI design knowledge, in their own terms, before attempting to apply those proposed here.

Difficult to complete?

Familiarise yourself with the main ways of characterising HCI craft artefacts and design practice experience, as HCI design knowledge, identified in the HCI design literature, before attempting to address those proposed here.

Test

List from memory as many of the section titles as you can.

5.5   NOTES

[1] Examples of best selling/most popular artefact lists follow.

Best Selling Web Browsers (2021)

1. Google Chrome

2. Apple Safari

3. Firefox

4. Microsoft Edge

Best Selling Gaming Consoles

1. Game Boy Advance
2. PSP
3. Xbox 360
4. PlayStation 3
5. Nintendo Wii
6. PlayStation
7. PlayStation 4
8. Game Boy/Colour
9. Nintendo DS
10. PlayStation 2

Most Popular Email Service Providers

1. Gmail
2. HubSpot
3. Sendinblue
4. ProtonMail
5. Outlook
6. Yahoo Mail
7. Zoho Mail
8. AOL Mail
9. Mail.com
10. GMX Mail
11. Cloud Mail
12. Yandex Mail

Most Popular E-Commerce Sites

1. Taobao
2. Amazon
3. Walmart
4. eBay
5. Target
6. Alibaba
7. Flipkart
8. NewEgg
9. Overstock
10. Best Buy

Best Free Email Accounts

1. Gmail
2. Outlook.com
3. Yahoo Mail
4. AOL Mail
5. Yandex Mail
6. ProtonMail
7. Zoho Mail
8. Tutanota
9. iCloud Mail
10. 10 Minute Mail

CHAPTER 6

HCI Design Knowledge as Models and Methods

SUMMARY

The chapter introduces models and methods as HCI design knowledge. The latter are exemplified in the form of "best-practice" in supporting design, either directly or indirectly, but in both cases explicitly. Some examples are taken from the two case studies of HCI-EDP acquisition, summarised in Chapter 9 and reported in full in the companion volume (Long et al., 2022, in press). Other examples are presented in contrast. All examples, as best-practice, could be used to acquire future HCI-EDPs. Also presented is a critique of HCI design knowledge, its current state and the associated challenge. Models and methods constitute one form of HCI design knowledge. They are acquired and validated explicitly by case studies solving the general HCI problem of design. The latter having the particular scope of humans interacting with computers to do something as desired. Both general question and particular scope are viewed from a discipline perspective. The introduction, as one type of HCI design knowledge, is preceded in the previous chapter on craft artefacts and design practice experience and followed in the subsequent chapter by principles, rules and heuristics, as other types of HCI design knowledge.

6.1   MODELS AND METHODS HCI DESIGN KNOWLEDGE

HCI design knowledge as models and methods, viewed from a discipline perspective, assumes HCI to be a discipline (see § 1.2) with a general problem (see § 1.2.1), a particular scope (see § 1.2.2) and which conducts HCI research (see § 2.3). Such models and methods are common forms of design knowledge, acquired and validated by HCI research, to support the practice of the design of humans interacting with computers to do something as desired (see also Long, 2021). The support may be more or less prescriptive, but is explicit. HCI models are an explicit representation of the "what" of HCI design, that is, the declarative product of application design. HCI methods are an explicit representation of the "how" of HCI design, that is, the procedural process of application design. The relationship is shown in Figure 6.1, which should be compared with Figures 1–5.1 for similarities and differences. Likewise, as a format for alternative conceptions, which readers might like to formulate for themselves.

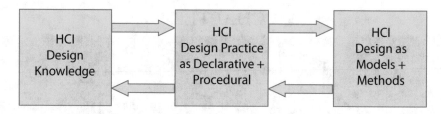

Figure 6.1: HCI design knowledge as models and methods.

For example, nuclear power station HCI models may include production targets, their limiting conditions and alarms, associated with violations of the production process. Multi-media HCI methods may include stages by which to specify verbal and image synthesisation for communication between air traffic controllers and pilots. Last, business-to-consumer HCI models and methods may include respectively the range, prices and quality of the goods for sale and the phases and stages by which they are specified in a customer order.

6.2   STATE OF MODELS HCI DESIGN KNOWLEDGE

Models, as HCI design knowledge, belong to a set of explicit frameworks and theories, espoused by interdisciplinary overlapping fields[1] (Rogers, 2012). The frameworks and theories are considered as HCI design knowledge, for present purposes, either if they form part of HCI frameworks or theories, with the potential of being used to support HCI design or if they have been used to support HCI design practice.

Historically, models have always been reported in the HCI research literature. One of the earliest examples is the cognitive psychology framework for interacting with the computer, proposed by Morton et al. (1979). They identify a technology industry model of users interacting with the computer, which is "computer-centric." In contrast, they propose "user-centric" models, expressed as block interaction, information structures, and state transition models. The models are intended to form the basis for design knowledge to support HCI designers. However, they are not themselves prescriptive with respect to design. A literature search fails to find any case studies reporting such support for design.

Perhaps the best-known models are those proposed by Card, Moran, and Newell (1983), as part of their psychology framework for HCI. They include a model of the user, interacting with the computer, in the form of the model human processor (MHP). It is an information processing-type model, following the psychology of the day. They also propose a family of models (GOMS). This stands for: Goals—that is desired aims to be achieved by the user; Operators—cognitive processes and physical actions needed to achieve the user's goals; Methods—that is steps and procedures to carry out the cognitive processes and physical actions, required to achieve the user's goals; and Selection Rules—that is by which the user is able to select the best method for achieving their goals. The models, as HCI design knowledge, are intended to form explicit and prescriptive support for HCI designers. Case studies include those of John and Gray (1995) and Teo and John (2008).

Barnard (1991), as part of his cognitive psychology-bridging framework, includes a family of cognitive task models, as associated with the interacting cognitive subsystems model. The models, as HCI design knowledge, are intended to constitute the basis of support for HCI designers in the form of engineering tools. The models themselves are explicit, however, they offer no explicit design prescription. A literature search fails to find any report of such tool development.

The state of models as HCI design knowledge can be illustrated in more detail by a model proposed by Smith et al. (1997) of the planning and control of multiple task work in secretarial office administration. The model itself is explicit, but does not offer explicit design prescription. However, it is referenced by the domestic energy planning and control case study for acquiring HCI-EDPs, summarised in Chapter 9.

Smith et al. (1997) propose a cognitive science-based, HCI design-oriented framework. The latter is for the planning and control of multiple task work in secretarial office administration. Multiple task work, here, refers to the performance of concurrent tasks by interactive human-computer systems. Secretarial office administration supports communications within organisations, including messaging, call answering and correspondence filing. The framework comprises models of the interactive system (both human and computer), its domain of secretarial work and the effectiveness, with which the work is carried out by the work system. The secretarial interactive system model expresses the relationship between abstract representations of the processes of planning, controlling, perceiving and executing. The model also expresses the abstract representations of plans and knowledge-of-tasks. Planning heuristics and control rules reflect general properties of the dynamic secretarial work domain, such as external interruptions and temporary opportunities. The framework also expresses the relationship between these planning and control structures and performance. Smith et al. argue that these models constitute putative HCI design knowledge and are intended to support designers in reasoning about potential solutions to HCI design problems, associated with the planning and control of multiple task work in secretarial office administration. No case study of such support has been identified to date.

Wright, Fields, and Harrison (2000) propose a resource model, as part of external cognition theory. The model comprises internal representations, for example, memorised procedures and external representations, such as written instructions. The model, as HCI design knowledge, is intended to support the work of HCI designers. The model is explicit, but offers no detailed design prescription. No associated application case study has been identified.

Kirsh (2001) proposes a model of "entry points," as part of ecological theory. The model comprises prompts, for example, by display structures, such as titles, columns, images, icons, tables, and figures. The latter invite appropriate interactive behaviours. Also proposed is a model of thinking with external representations. Both models, as HCI design knowledge claim, support the work of HCI designers. The model is explicit, but offers no direct design prescription. No associated application case study has been identified.

The state of models, as HCI design knowledge, can also be illustrated in more detail by a model for expressing the effectiveness of planning horizons, proposed by Timmer and Long (2002), referenced by the domestic energy planning and control case study for acquiring HCI-EDPs (summarised in Chapter 9). They make explicit a number of critical relationships, which are required, before the expression of the effectiveness of planning horizons in air traffic management can be formulated.

Espousing the HCI engineering discipline framework of Long and Dowell (1989) and the HCI general design problem framework of Dowell and Long (1989), they propose the "theory of the operator planning horizon" (TOPH) to identify the behavioural phenomena, associated with controller planning horizon effectiveness. The theory supports the explicit derivation of data requirements, which form the basis for a representation of such a horizon. In a similar vein, the domain model enables the identification of problems of interactive worksystem performance. It also supports the subsequent construction of an interactive worksystem (sic) model to identify the behaviour responsible for the unacceptable quality of the traffic management work. Establishing relationships from the data, the method, serves to augment the subjective (and anecdotal) recall of operator "problems" with technologies. In addition, the relationships offer a basis for quantifying problems and the subsequent formulation of re-design priorities.

Timmer and Long claim the method to be a useful tool, to complement existing HCI design knowledge and practices, for the explicit expression of design problems. As such, it is considered to advance HCI design knowledge. They conclude, that in the absence of a well-specified expression of the design problem, there can be no known design solution and so no acquisition and validation of HCI design knowledge supporting the transition from one to the other. The TOPH worksystem model is shown in Figure 6.2. It illustrates the Reconstructed Air Traffic Management worksystem and, in addition, serves to illustrate the HCI design models of this section more generally. The model is explicit, but offers no detailed design prescription. Long and Hill (2005) report a validation case study of TOPH.

Carroll (2003 and 2010), as part of his science framework, proposes models as concern scenario-based design and the associated design rationale. Both types of model, as HCI design knowledge, are proposed to support the work of HCI designers. For scenario-based case studies see Carroll, Kellog, and Rosson (1991).

The models referenced so far as HCI design knowledge form part of HCI frameworks. HCI theories, however, also include models as potential or actual HCI design knowledge.

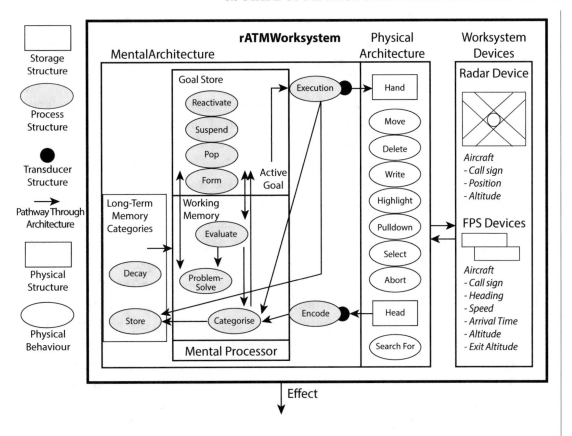

Figure 6.2: Model of Reconstructed Air Traffic Management Worksystem (following Timmer and Long, 2002).

6.3   STATE OF METHODS HCI DESIGN KNOWLEDGE

Methods, as HCI design knowledge, belong to a set of explicit frameworks and theories, espoused by interdisciplinary overlapping fields[1] (Rogers, 2012). The frameworks and theories are considered as HCI design knowledge, for present purposes, either if they have already been used to support HCI design practice or if they have the potential of being used to support HCI design.

Glaser and Strauss (1967), as part of grounded theory, propose a method by which such theories may be developed on the basis of data, its acquisition and its analysis. The method is intended for application by HCI designers. For an example of its case study application, see Denley and Long later.

Lim and Long (1994) propose a method, which espouses an engineering framework. The method is entitled MUSE. It provides explicit and prescriptive support for HCI interaction designers. MUSE is a structured analysis and design method, originally intended for application with Jackson System Development (JSD), a software engineering development method. In practice, it can be used with most software engineering development methods. The reference includes a number of case studies.

Phase 1 is termed the Information Elicitation and Analysis Phase. It requires the collection and analysis of user, device, and task information in support of subsequent design.

Phase 2 is termed the Design Synthesis Phase. The latter identifies, in terms of client criteria, such as performance, the end-user requirements to be achieved by the to-be-designed interactive system. Using the latter information and the user, device and task models from the first phase, a conceptual design is specified in the form of structured diagrams. The conceptual specification is agreed with the software engineering design team. The conceptual design is next divided into those tasks to be performed, using the interactive system under development, from those performed using other devices. An allocation of function between user and interactive computer is then carried out.

Phase 3 and the final phase is termed the Design Specification Phase. The conceptual design is decomposed further to create an interactive device-specific, implementable specification, which includes support for error-recovery. The interactive user interface is then evaluated and iteratively developed further. Once client performance criteria are met or are at least acceptable to the client, the interface design is passed to the software engineering design team for implementation.

The MUSE method is shown in Figure 6.3. It illustrates the method itself and, in addition, serves to illustrate the HCI design methods of this section more generally.

Denley and Long (2001) propose a method to support HCI design. The method supports multidisciplinary practice in requirements engineering (RE). They argue that multidisciplinary requirements engineering practice is ineffective and that some specific problems can be identified. They also suggest that the incommensurability of conflicting paradigms (ICP) is an underlying cause of these problems. Criteria for the successful address of such problems are presented. Denley and Long propose a method (ICP/RE) to address the incommensurability of conflicting paradigms. It takes the form of a dialectic process and its associated products. The latter are conceptualised and then operationalised. The latter is conducted for two different requirements engineering methods from two different discipline perspectives (representing two different paradigms, according to the authors), in the domain of accident and emergency healthcare. The methods are MUSE (Lim and Long, 1994) and grounded theory (Glaser and Strauss, 1967). For both methods—see earlier. The ICP/RE method is explicit, but offers no other detailed design prescription other than itself.

Shneiderman (2010), as part of direct manipulation theory, proposes a method, which includes three basic design prescriptions. First, digital object representations and their associated actions should be continuous (to reduce users' memory load). Second, such actions should be rapid, reversible, and incremental and be followed by immediate feedback (to support error recovery). Third, such actions should be embodied physically. The method, as HCI design knowledge, is intended for application by HCI designers. The method is explicit and instances design prescription. Case study illustrations are reported by the reference.

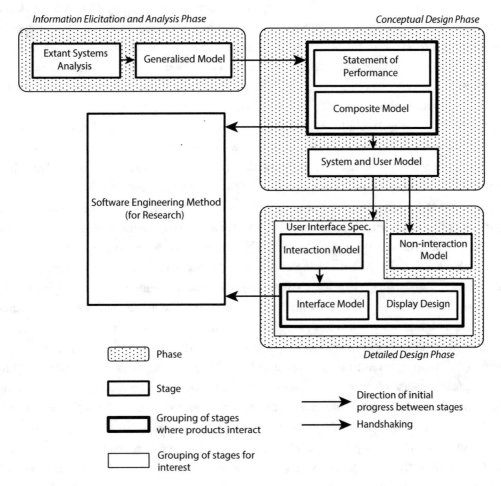

Figure 6.3: MUSE (following Lim and Long, 1994).

6.4   STATE OF MODELS AND METHODS HCI DESIGN KNOWLEDGE

Models and methods, as HCI design knowledge, belong to a set of explicit frameworks and theories, espoused by interdisciplinary overlapping fields[1] (Rogers, 2012). The frameworks and theories are considered as HCI design knowledge, for present purposes, if they form part of HCI frameworks or theories, either if they have been used to support HCI design practice or if they have the potential of being used to support HCI design.

Carroll (2003 and 2010) proposes a conceptualisation for HCI. This includes design rationale both as a framework and as a theory. The function of the theory is to integrate research and practice. Design rationale supports a description of the history and meaning of an artefact. Carroll claims that the most effective way forward for science in HCI design, such as applied cognitive science, is to interpret successful designs being used in practice. The interpretation is then "codified" as the knowledge, implicit in those designs in the form of models of claims identification and design rationale. The latter can be applied explicitly in subsequent designs, for example, by means of the scenario-based method. The method is intended for application by designers. Importing these insights into HCI design, according to Carroll, would constitute theory-based design. The models and method are explicit and prescriptive. Case studies are reported by the references.

Rauterberg (2006) espouses the frameworks of Long and Dowell (1989) and Dowell and Long (1989). This includes the worksystem (a term used by the references), the work domain, and performance as task quality and user costs. The framework supports a research-line, including its triangulation, that is validation of design knowledge as theory and its empirical evaluation. Rauterberg argues that to become an engineering discipline, HCI needs a well-specified interaction space. The latter requires a method to include—problems, a coherent taxonomy, a rigorous validation method, a coherent scientific language to achieve consensus, and a research-line to develop validated design knowledge. The method is intended for use by HCI designers. The models and method are explicit, but detailed design prescription is not offered. Illustrative case studies are referenced.

Dowell (1998) claims that evolutionary approaches to the cognitive design of air traffic management (ATM) systems can be held responsible for a history of delayed development. An example of the latter is the case of the flight progress strip. Attempts to design a computer-based system replacement for the paper strip have consistently failed to meet with acceptance and so have never been implemented. Dowell argues for an alternative approach. His proposal is also based on the formulation of cognitive design problems, following the HCI engineering framework of Dowell and Long (1989). Both the latter and Dowell (1998) are referenced by the domestic energy planning and control case study for the acquisition of HCI-EDPs, summarised in Chapter 9.

Dowell's research demonstrates how a cognitive design problem can be formulated for a simulated ATM task performed by controller subjects. The design problem is formulated in terms of two complementary models. The first is of the ATM domain, which represents the cognitive task environment of managing the simulated air traffic. The second model is of the ATM worksystem (his term), which represents the abstract cognitive behaviours of the controllers and their devices in performing the traffic management task. Taken together, the models provide a statement of worksystem performance and express the cognitive design problem for the simulated system. Dowell instantiates a method for design problem formulation. He argues further for the use of design problem formulation to be integrated into cognitive design methods, as HCI design knowledge, to support the design of computer-based flight strips and interactive systems more generally. The models and method are explicit, but the prescribed integration is not reported.

Hill's research (2010) espouses the HCI engineering discipline and design problem frameworks of Long and Dowell (1989) and Dowell and Long (1989), respectively. The models and method are explicit, but offer no complete design prescriptions, only example illustrations. However, the research is referenced by the domestic energy planning and control case study for acquiring HCI-EDPs, summarised in Chapter 9. Hill applies the frameworks to model the UK national system for the co-ordination of the emergency services in response to disasters, that is the Emergency Management Combined Response System (EMCRS). The latter is a complex three-tier command and control system. It was originally set up in response to the need for more effective co-ordination between agencies such as police, ambulance, and fire services, in their joint response to disasters.

To support HCI design practice, Hill proposes models of the EMCRS, as HCI design knowledge. These include the interactive system, comprising abstract structures of planning and control and physical structures of user and devices. The models also include the abstract interactive system structures of the specific domain of application. The models, as design knowledge, are intended to support HCI designers to diagnose design problems, associated with co-ordination between agencies. Data for the models were acquired from the observation and documentation of EMCRS training exercises. Co-ordination problems are identified on the basis of behaviour conflicts between the agencies. For example, the fire service behaviours of setting up a cordon around the disaster site conflict with the ambulance service behaviours of accessing the site for the treatment of casualties.

The EMCRS models, as HCI design knowledge, support design practice, as the diagnosis of design problems and indirectly, as support for the proposed prescription of design solutions. The Hill model is shown in Figure 6.4, followed by the Hill method. Together, they illustrate the model and method themselves and, in addition, they serve to exemplify the HCI design models and methods of this section more generally.

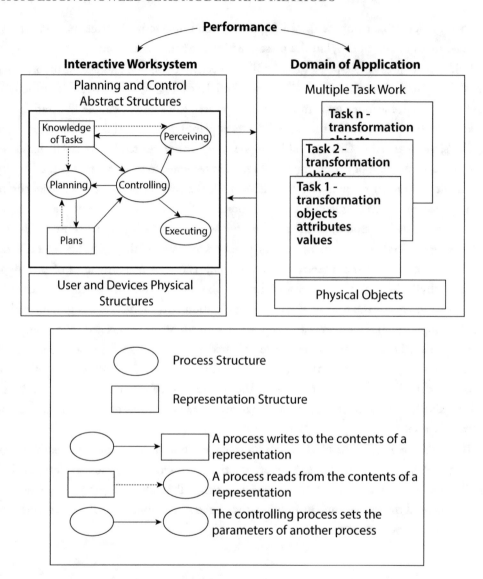

Figure 6.4: Performance expressed in terms of interactive worksystem and domain of application (following Hill, 2010).

The Hill method, expressed as actions and illustrations follows.

- Stage 1

    ○ Action: From data, identify tasks carried out by each agency in response to the scenario, where there are potential conflicts.

- ○ Illustration: Set-up of inner cordon by the Fire Service; access to casualties for triage without regulation safety equipment by the Ambulance Service.

- Stage 2

  - ○ Action: Use Model 1 to describe the behaviours associated with each task and the corresponding desired domain sub-object transformations.

  - ○ Illustration: Desired domain sub-object transformations are those transformations that would be carried out, if an agency's behaviours were not hindered. For the above example, one desired domain sub-object transformation for the Ambulance Service would be: Lives sub-object attribute survivor triage status from untriaged to triaged.

- Stage 3

  - ○ Action: Identify behaviour conflicts, that is, which domain sub-object transformations will hinder other domain sub-object transformations.

  - ○ Illustration: From the above example, the Fire Service behaviours of transforming the Disaster Scene sub-object attribute scene containment from un-contained to contained have hindered the Ambulance Service behaviours and corresponding domain sub-object transformations

- Stage 4

  - ○ Action: Use Model 1 to identify whether other domain sub-object transformations will be hindered as a "knock-on effect" from the initial conflict behaviour.

  - ○ Illustration: For example, the Ambulance Service not being able to transform the Lives sub-object attribute survivor triage status from untriaged to triaged will mean that the Lives sub-object attribute survivor treatment status cannot be transformed from not treated to treated. Also, as the Ambulance Service cannot access the casualties, the Fire Service will have to move the casualties to the edge of the cordon to enable triage to take place. In so doing, the Fire Service will reduce their fire fighting and property protection behaviours, as personnel will need to be taken away from these tasks to carry out rescue behaviours and will therefore not be able to transform the Disaster Character sub-object attribute fire status from uncontrolled to controlled, and the Property sub-object attributes of buildings/vehicles status from at risk to not at risk.

- Stage 5

  - ○ Action: Identify the performance effect of the hindered domain sub-object transformations by referring to the overall common objectives and priorities of the EMCRS (that is, to save life, to prevent escalation of the disaster, etc.). The primary priority for all services is to save life. Therefore, hindering any domain sub-object transformation that reduces life saving by the EMCRS will have the greatest impact on performance.

  - ○ Illustration: In the current example, hindering triage and subsequent treatment transformations by the Ambulance Service, of the Lives sub-object will greatly affect the performance of the EMCRS with respect to the primary priority of saving life. Reducing the fire fighting and property protection behaviours by the Fire Service will have an effect on the secondary priority of preventing escalation of the disaster. Thus, Model 1 gives a performance expression of actual performance being less than planned/ desired performance, as a performance deficit, shown for both agencies.

6.5   CRITIQUE AND CHALLENGE FOR MODELS AND METHODS HCI DESIGN KNOWLEDGE

HCI models and methods,[2] as HCI design knowledge, constitute one form of HCI discipline knowledge. Such models and methods are acquired by HCI research. They may embody both diagnostic and prescriptive HCI design knowledge. The latter is intended to support HCI practitioners in the design of interactive systems as desired. HCI discipline knowledge, including that of models and methods, is to be judged by the effectiveness of that support. Simply to conceptualise the latter offers by itself no assurance as to the effectiveness of models and methods. Their conceptualisation alone is unable to provide such assurance. The challenge, then, for HCI design knowledge in general, including for HCI models and methods in particular, is how to ensure the effectiveness of the knowledge, which they offer in support of HCI design. The effectiveness for this purpose can be considered for models and methods both as concerns their acquisition, their validation and the relations between them. For example, very general models and methods may be easier to conceptualise but the conceptualisation may be harder to operationalise, test, and generalise and so validate explicitly. Unvalidated or poorly validated design knowledge is unable to provide the assurance required for reliable support of HCI design.

For example, the model and method illustrations in § 6.4 appear not to set any limits for the application of their associated HCI design knowledge as concerns its design problems, its interactive system user and computer behaviours and its level of description. The individual models and methods appear to be intended for general application. However, such generality does not necessarily favour the effectiveness of that application. Indeed, as suggested earlier, it may even militate against it.

For example, Dowell (1998) appears to make no distinction between the abstract cognitive behaviours of the controllers and their devices in performing the traffic management task. The models and method, then, may be overly powerful with respect to these abstract cognitive behaviours and so harder to validate as a result. This is not known, but cannot be excluded. Hence, it remains a challenge of how to make Dowell's models and method more effective in their support for design.

For example, Timmer and Long (2002) conclude, that in the absence of a well-specified expression of a design problem, there can be no known design solution, nor acquisition and validation of HCI design knowledge supporting the transition from one to the other. However, they do not propose criteria for how well specified design problems need to be for the specification to be appropriate for the acquisition and validation of HCI design knowledge. The appropriateness of the specification of such knowledge, then, remains a challenge for the effectiveness of their model and method in the latter's support for design.

For example, Carroll's scenario-based design method (2003 and 2010) appears to make no distinction between the design problems to which it is intended to be applied. The method, then, may be overly powerful with respect to these problems and so easier to conceptualise; but harder to validate as a result. This is not known; but cannot be excluded. Hence, it remains part of the challenge of how to make Carroll's method more effective in its support for design. The same can be said of Rauterberg's vigorous validation method (2006), which also appears to make no distinction between design problems to which it might be applied.

Last, for example, Hill (2010) claims that the Emergency Management Combined Response System (EMCRS) models, as HCI design knowledge, support design practice, as the diagnosis of design problems and indirectly, as support for the proposed prescription of design solutions. These claims are accepted, at least as far as EMCRS design problems are concerned. However, there is no evidence or explicit claim that the models and methods can be applied to design problems in other domains. Again, the claims may be overly powerful and so difficult to operationalise in such domains. This likewise applies to the support for the prescription of design solutions, which is in any case only indirect, even in the case of EMCRS design.

No attempt is made here to characterise how this challenge to HCI models and methods might be met. The requirement is simply to identify the challenge. However, how HCI-EDPs might meet the challenge is proposed in Chapters 8 and 9, together with some ideas of how models and methods might also meet the challenge.

REVIEW

The chapter characterises models and methods as actual or potential explicit HCI design knowledge, supporting design more or less prescriptively. It also describes and critiques their current state and identifies the associated challenge. Models and methods constitute a form of HCI design knowledge. The latter is acquired and validated explicitly by case studies to solve the general HCI problem of design with the particular scope of humans interacting with computers to do something as desired, as viewed from a discipline perspective. The latter is espoused here for the development of HCI-EDPs. The introduction, as one type of HCI design knowledge—models and methods—is followed in the subsequent chapter by another type of design knowledge in the form of principles, rules and heuristics.

6.6   PRACTICE ASSIGNMENT

Practice Assignment 6.1.

Describe the assumptions made by your research as concerns—HCI design models (see § 6.2), HCI design methods (see § 6.3) and conjoint HCI design models and methods (see § 6.4), as HCI design knowledge to support HCI design practice. If you have no research of your own at this time, select suitable research of a colleague or supervisor/instructor/teacher. Alternatively, select a suitable publication from the HCI research literature.

- Contrast the similarities and differences between the assumptions made by your (or that of other's) research and the proposals made here.

- How might the differences be made coherent?

- If they cannot be made coherent, why might this be so?

Hints and Tips

Difficult to get started?

Try reading the chapter again, while at the same time thinking about how to describe your own (or that of others) HCI design models and methods, as HCI design knowledge. Note similarities and differences between the two lines of thought, as you go along.

- Describe your (or that of others) HCI design models and methods, as HCI design knowledge, in its own terms, before attempting to apply those proposed here.

Difficult to complete?

Familiarise yourself with the main ways of conceptualising HCI models and methods, as HCI design knowledge, identified in the HCI literature, before attempting to address those proposed here.

Test

List from memory as many of the section titles as you can.

Practice Assignment 6.2.

List all the references in Chapter 6 for models, for methods and for models and methods, which are claimed to have no related case studies at the time of going to press. Search the HCI literature for case studies, which may have been reported since then. Assess the latter for coherence, completeness, and fitness-for-purpose, as concerns the claims made by the individual case study. The aim of the assignment is to familiarise the reader with case studies in general, their associated claims, and the appropriateness of the latter.

Practice Assignment 6.3.

List all the references in Chapter 6 for models, for methods, and for models and methods, as design knowledge, which are claimed to have been applied in the HCI-EDP summaries, presented in Chapter 9. Check the application as reported, such that you understand how this design knowledge has been applied. Assess informally, whether you think other models, methods, and models and methods not applied in the case studies, could be equally well applied in the acquisition of future HCI-EDPs.

6.7   NOTES

[1] Rogers' (2012) complete set of interdisciplinary overlapping fields comprises—human factors, cognitive engineering, human-computer interaction, cognitive ergonomics, computer-supported cooperative work (CSCW), and information systems.

[2] Note that the scope of HCI models and methods, as HCI design knowledge, characterised as a set of explicit research practices of acquisition and validation, espoused by interdisciplinary overlapping fields is to be contrasted with the scope of HCI research as a set of both implicit and explicit research practices of acquisition and validation, espoused by interdisciplinary overlapping fields (Rogers, 2012). For example, cognitive engineering HCI research practices of acquisition and validation involve explicit codified knowledge as models and methods. Graphic design research practices of acquisition and validation, however, are likely to include implicit knowledge as models and methods, embodied in the design practice experience of the designer. For this reason, it would be inappropriate to address the latter for present purposes other than principally as craft design (see § 5.1–2).

CHAPTER 7

HCI Design Knowledge as Principles, Rules, and Heuristics

SUMMARY

The chapter introduces principles, rules and heuristics as HCI design knowledge. The latter are exemplified in the form of "best-practice" in supporting design. The support may be prescriptive and may be explicit. Some examples are applied in the two case studies of HCI-EDP acquisition, summarised in Chapter 9 and reported in full in the companion volume (Long et al., 2022, in press). Other examples, as best-practice, could be used to acquire future HCI-EDPs. Also presented is a critique of HCI design knowledge, its current state, and the associated challenge. Principles, rules, and heuristics constitute one form of HCI design knowledge. They are acquired and can be validated explicitly by case studies solving the general HCI problem of design. The latter having the particular scope of humans interacting with computers to do something as desired. Both general question and particular scope are viewed from a discipline perspective. The introduction, presenting one type of HCI design knowledge, is preceded in previous chapters by craft artefacts and design practice experience and models and methods, as other types of HCI design knowledge. The following chapter presents HCI-EDP design knowledge.

7.1 PRINCIPLES, RULES, AND HEURISTICS DESIGN KNOWLEDGE

In general, principles are considered to constitute a basic component of discipline knowledge at least for the disciplines of science and engineering. Depending on the discipline, principles may take the form of truth proposition, law, prescription, doctrine, or theory. Likewise for rules, in general, which may take the form of guidelines, action prescription and strategy. Likewise for heuristics, in general, which may take the form of hints and tips, examples, and experience. However, when viewed from a discipline perspective, in all cases, principles, rules, and heuristics serve as the object of HCI research as the acquisition and the validation of implicit or explicit prescriptive discipline knowledge to support design practice. Principles, rules and heuristics are distinguished here in terms of their prescriptive force and their implicit/explicit expression. Principles, rules and heuristics then, embody the purpose of HCI discipline knowledge, which is to support HCI discipline practice. The relationship is shown in Figure 7.1, which should be compared with Figures 1–6.1 for similarities and differences. Likewise, as a format for alternative conceptions, which readers might like to formulate for themselves.

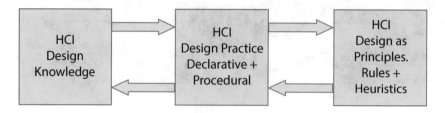

Figure 7.1: HCI design knowledge as principles, rules, and heuristics.

7.2   STATE OF HCI PRINCIPLES, RULES, AND HEURISTICS DESIGN KNOWLEDGE

The states of HCI principles, rules, and heuristics are addressed in turn.

7.2.1   PRINCIPLES HCI DESIGN KNOWLEDGE

Wickens principles (1984 and 1993[1]) are an example of principles HCI design knowledge. They are based on human factors research and apply to display design, including HCI display design. They constitute one of the first expressions of HCI design principles. They are both prescriptive and explicit. They are referenced in many HCI textbooks. Their contribution to HCI is widely acknowledged. However, it is time to question their current status.

The Wickens principles appear in a number of publications and are generally considered to include the following.

1.   Make display legible/audible.

2.   Avoid absolute judgment limits.

3.   Top-down processing.

4.   Redundancy gain.

5.   Discriminability. Similarity causes confusion: use discriminable elements.

6.   Principle of pictorial realism.

7.   Principle of moving part.

8.   Minimising information access cost.

9.   Proximity compatibility principle.

10. Principle of multiple resources.

This principle is something to do with multimodality. Two information sources, visually and auditorily, can more easily be perceived than using both visual channels. For example, a navigation map showing a city name and speech saying "you are 500 meters from your destination" are easily perceived compared to putting the "500 meters from your destination" as a text over the map.

11. Replace memory with visual information: knowledge in the world.

This principle can be called that of ecological display. Showing something that directly resembles what's happening in the real world. The more similar to the real world, the more informative it is and the user can more easily decode the information.

12. Principle of predictive aiding.

13. Principle of consistency.

This principle is somehow related to long-term memory information. Previous knowledge of a certain way of information display would be used again when users meet another information display of the same signal. Using a commonly known display element/symbol in order to convey different information, simply would not work.

If the Wickens principles constitute the basic elements of HCI design knowledge, then as well as being conceptualised, they also need to be operationalised, tested, and generalised, that is validated (see § 1.2.3.1–2). Validation may be either formal, for example, by experimental or simulation evaluation or informal, for example, by personal or team design experience. Wickens, to give him credit, does not make such a claim. Nor does he appear to recognise such a requirement. Further, examination of the principles in detail (for example, Principles 10, 11, and 13) suggests that their conceptual underspecification renders them difficult to operationalise for the purposes of assessment and generalisation. Although not necessarily to be applied by individual, as opposed to team, design. In other words, they cannot be validated other than by experience as they stand. Readers might like to try operationalising for themselves, in whichever way they choose, the italicised words in the following principles:

- Principle 10: This principle is something to do with multimodality.

- Principle 11: This principle can be called that of *ecological* display.

- Principle 13: This principle is *somehow* related to long-term memory information.

Readers should now consider how difficult it might be to persuade other design team members of their preferred operationalisation.

This is not to say that the Wickens principles cannot be of use to HCI designers. Only that their support for HCI design offers no more assurance, as concerns their effectiveness in this respect, than that offered, for example, by heuristics. The latter typically constituting little more than design "hints and tips." HCI designers might do well to keep the Wickens principles in mind, if they work for them, when designing. Also, to make the best sense and use of them as they can. In that case, however, any advantage accruing to the design as a result would depend on the imagination, interpretation and experience of the designer and their design team as much, or even more so, than on the application of the principle-cum-heuristic itself. Either way, it would not be explicitly known and so communicable to others, more generally. It is clear, however, that the Wickens principles do not offer the assurance of effective HCI knowledge, as required by an HCI discipline perspective, to support HCI practitioners to specify and to implement interactive system designs as desired. Exactly the same argument can be advanced with respect to such principles of other researchers (see later), as is applied to those of Wickens.

It might be argued that the Wickens principles are intended only for displays and not for interactive human-computer systems more generally. Also, that the origin of the principles is human factors engineering research, rather than HCI research. Both arguments, however, are rejected. The declared scope of the Wickens principles is displays. The latter are generally interactive, at least to some extent. Further, interactive displays were and continue to be part of interactive systems. Last, it might be argued, that Wickens never claimed assurance for the effectiveness of his principles. There is no disagreement there, then. However, this does not change the assessment of the current state of the Wickens principles offered here.

The Norman principles are also an example of principles as HCI design knowledge. Norman's HCI principles (1983, 1986, and 2013[1]) are generally considered to include the following.

1.   Use both knowledge in the world and knowledge in the head.

2.   Simplify the structure of tasks.

3.   Make things visible.

4.   Get the mappings right.

5.   Exploit the power of constraints, both natural and artificial.

6.   Design for error.

7.   When all else fails, standardise.

If the Norman principles constitute the basic elements of HCI discipline knowledge, then as well as being conceptualised, they also need to be operationalised, tested, and generalised (see § 1.2.3.1–2), at least from the discipline perspective, adopted here. Norman makes no such claim nor recognises such a requirement. Further, examination of the principles suggests that their conceptual underspecification renders them difficult to operationalise for the purposes of explicit testing and to generalise. As they stand, then, they cannot be shown to be explicitly validated and so known, other than by design experience.

However, the latter offers no more assurance, as concerns their effectiveness in this respect, than that offered by the principles-cum-heuristics of Wickens, as design "hints and tips."

Readers might like to try operationalising for themselves the italicised words in the following principles.

- Principle 2. *Simplify the structure* of tasks.

- Principle 4. Get the mappings *right*.

- Principle 5. Exploit the *power* of constraints, both natural and artificial.

Readers should now consider how difficult it might be to persuade other design team members of their preferred operationalisation.

Again, as with the Wickens principles, this is not to say that the Norman principles cannot be of use to HCI designers. Only that the principles are no more than heuristics or "hints and tips." HCI designers might do well to keep them in mind, when designing interactive human-computer systems. However, any contribution to the resulting design would depend on the designer or design team as much, or even more than, on the application of the principle-cum-heuristic itself. It is, however, clear that the Norman principles-cum-heuristics do not offer the assurance of effective knowledge, as required by the HCI discipline, to support practitioners to specify and to implement interactive system designs as desired. It might be argued, that Norman never claimed such assurance. Indeed, the semi-humorous tone of Principle 7. "When all else fails, standardise" suggests that he himself was well aware that such assurance is lacking. There is no disagreement there, then. The same argument, as advanced for the Norman principles, can be applied to the principles proposed by other researchers.

As concerns HCI knowledge, the following claims are made here. First, that HCI principles should be different from heuristics. Second, that the difference between HCI principles and HCI heuristics should be the greater assurance, that the former offers with respect to the effectiveness of the application of HCI knowledge to support design. Third, that HCI principles in general and the specific HCI principles analysed (those of Wickens and Norman) are more akin to heuristics than to principles.

7.2.2   RULES HCI DESIGN KNOWLEDGE

The Shneiderman rules (1983 and 1998[2]) are an example of rule HCI design knowledge. Shneiderman proposes "golden" rules intended to support interactive system design. They are both prescriptive and explicit. They are the best known and widely referenced of such rules. Across various publications, they are generally considered to include the following:

1.   Strive for consistency.

2.   Enable frequent users to use shortcuts.

3.   Offer informative feedback.

4.   Design dialogs to yield closure.

5.   Offer error prevention and simple error handling.

6.   Permit easy reversal of actions.

7.   Support internal locus of control.

8.   Reduce short-term memory load.

If the Shneiderman rules form the basic elements of HCI discipline design knowledge, then like principles they also need to be operationalised, tested, and generalised from a discipline perspective (see § 1.2.3.1–2). Shneiderman makes no such claim nor recognises any such requirement. Further, examination of the rules suggests that their conceptual underspecification renders them difficult to support operationalisation and so test and generalisation. The rules, then, cannot be explicitly validated, as they stand. Readers might like to try operationalising for themselves the italicised words in the following principles.

4. Design dialogs to yield *closure*.

7. Support internal *locus of control*.

8. Reduce *short-term memory load*.

Readers should now consider how difficult it might be to persuade other design team members of their preferred operationalisation.

Again, as with principles, this is not to say, that the Shneiderman rules cannot be of help to HCI designers. Only that the rules are no more than "hints and tips," that is to say heuristics. HCI designers might do well to keep them in mind. However, any contribution to interactive system design would depend as much or even more on the experience and imagination of the designer or the design team members than on the rule itself. Yet, it is clear that the Shneiderman rules-cum-heuristics do not offer the assurance of effective HCI knowledge to support HCI practitioners in the specification and implementation of interactive systems as desired. It might be argued, that Shneiderman never claimed such assurance. There is no disagreement there, then. Exactly the same argument can be advanced with respect to the application by researchers of rules other than those of Shneiderman.

The three propositions, made earlier, concerning HCI principles can now be re-iterated for HCI rules. First, that HCI rules should be different from heuristics. Second, that the difference between HCI rules and heuristics should be the greater reassurance that the former offers with respect to the effectiveness of the application of HCI discipline knowledge to support design. Third, that HCI rules in general and the specific rules analysed, that is, those of Shneiderman, are more akin to heuristics than to rules.

Further support for the preceding propositions would accrue, if HCI heuristics were also not to be different from HCI principles or HCI rules, as propagated in the HCI research literature. Nielsen proposes 10 heuristics (1993, 1994a, and 1994b), intended to support interactive system design (see § 7.2.3). They are perhaps the best known and widely referenced of all the HCI heuristics. They make a suitable comparison, then, with HCI principles and rules to establish, whether there is in practice any difference in the usage of these three descriptors for basic HCI discipline knowledge.

7.2.3   HEURISTICS HCI DESIGN KNOWLEDGE

The Nielsen heuristics are an example of heuristic HCI design knowledge. Nielsen[3] proposes 10 basic heuristics to support HCI interactive human-computer system design. They are both prescriptive and explicit. They are the best known and widely referenced of such heuristics. The Nielsen heuristics are as follows:

1.   Visibility of system status.

    The system should always keep users informed about what is going on, through appropriate feedback within reasonable time.

2.   Match between system and the real world.

    The system should speak the user's language, with words, phrases, and concepts familiar to the user, rather than system-oriented terms. Follow real-world conventions, making information appear in a natural and logical order.

3.   User control and freedom.

    Users often choose system functions by mistake and will need a clearly marked "emergency exit" to leave the unwanted state without having to go through an extended dialogue. Support undo and redo.

4.   Consistency and standards.

Users should not have to wonder whether different words, situations, or actions mean the same thing. Follow platform conventions.

5. Error prevention.

    Even better than good error messages is careful design, which prevents a problem from occurring in the first place. Either eliminate error-prone conditions or check for them and present users with a confirmation option before they commit to the action.

6. Recognition rather than recall.

    Minimise the user's memory load by making objects, actions, and options visible. The user should not have to remember information from one part of the dialogue to another. Instructions for use of the system should be visible or easily retrievable whenever appropriate.

7. Flexibility and efficiency of use.

    Accelerators—unseen by the novice user—may often speed up the interaction for the expert user such that the system can cater to both inexperienced and experienced users. Allow users to tailor frequent actions.

8. Aesthetic and minimalist design.

    Dialogues should not contain information, which is irrelevant or rarely needed. Every extra unit of information in a dialogue competes with the relevant units of information and diminishes their relative visibility.

9. Help users recognise, diagnose, and recover from errors.

    Error messages should be expressed in plain language (no codes), precisely indicate the problem, and constructively suggest a solution.

10. Help and documentation.

    Even though it is better, if the system can be used without documentation, it may be necessary to provide help and documentation. Any such information should be easy to search, focussed on the user's task, list concrete steps to be carried out, and not be too large.

As heuristics, HCI designers might do well to keep them in mind. However, it is clear that the Nielsen heuristics do not offer any assurance of the effectiveness of HCI knowledge to support HCI practitioners in the specification and implementation of interactive systems as desired. It might be argued that Nielsen, as appropriate for heuristics, never claimed such assurance. There is no disagreement there, then. Exactly the same argument can be advanced with respect to the application by researchers of heuristics other than those of Nielsen.

7.3   CRITIQUE AND CHALLENGE FOR HCI PRINCIPLES, RULES, AND HEURISTICS DESIGN KNOWLEDGE

To be validated, principles, rules, and heuristics, albeit in different ways, need to be conceptualised, operationalised, tested, and generalised (see § 1.2.3.1–2) from a discipline perspective. Conceptualisation has been shown earlier for the principles of Wickens and Norman, the rules of Shneiderman and the heuristics of Nielsen. Hence, a relative comparison between the conceptualisations is possible. The interest of such a comparison resides in the expected difference between them. Principles and rules would be expected to be more clearly identified, more complete and more coherent than heuristics. If so, principles and rules might be considered to exhibit greater potential than the heuristics to offer the assurance, concerning the effectiveness of HCI design knowledge, as required by HCI.

First, consider the clarity with which the concepts of the principles, rules and heuristics are identified. To facilitate the comparison, similar principles/heuristics have been selected—Wickens Principle 11, Norman Principle 1, Shneiderman Rule 7, and Nielsen Heuristic 2. In all cases, the content concerns the relationship between the "real world," the user's knowledge of the "real world," the locus of control and the interactive system's representation of the "real" world. The recommendations are as follows.

- Wickens

    Principle 11. Replace memory with visual information: knowledge in the world.

    This can be called the principle of ecological display. Showing something that directly resembles what's happening on the real world. The more similar to the real world, the more informative it is and the user can more easily decode the information.

- Norman

    Principle 1. Use both knowledge in the world and knowledge in the head.

- Shneiderman

    Rule 7. Support internal locus of control.

- Nielsen

    Heuristic 2. Match between system and the real world.

The system should speak the users' language, with words, phrases and concepts familiar to the user, rather than system-oriented terms. Follow real-world conventions, making information appear in a natural and logical order.

Readers can confirm for themselves, that there is no discernable difference between the clarity with which the concepts of principle, rule, and heuristic are identified. Indeed, their expressions, although not quite identical, are clearly similar and comparable. No greater clarity of concept identification by the principles and rules over heuristics is observed.

Second, consider the completeness and coherence with which the concepts of the principles and rules versus the heuristics are expressed. To facilitate the comparison, similar principles/heuristics have been selected—Wickens Principle 13, Norman Principle 5, Shneiderman Rule 1 and Nielsen Heuristic 4. In all cases, the content concerns (sometimes different) aspects of consistency. The concepts are as follows:

- Wickens

  Principle 13. Principle of consistency.

  This principle is somehow related to long-term memory information. Previous knowledge of a certain way of information display would be used again when users meet another information display of the same signal. Using a commonly known display element/symbol in order to convey different information, simply would not work.

- Norman

  Principle 5. Exploit the power of constraints, both natural and artificial.

- Shneiderman

  Rule 1. Strive for consistency.

- Nielsen

  Heuristic 4. Consistency and standards.

  Users should not have to wonder whether different words, situations, or actions mean the same thing. Follow platform conventions.

Readers can confirm for themselves, that there is no discernable difference between the completeness and coherence with which the concepts of principle, rule, and heuristic are described. Indeed, their expressions, although not identical, are clearly similar and comparable, that is at the same level of description. No greater completeness or coherence of concept description by the principles and the rules over the heuristics is observed.

Third, consider the potential of principle, rule, and heuristic for operationalisation, test, and generalisation, given their conceptualisation. Such potential would normally be difficult to assess. However, in the present case it is easy. Since no discernable differences between principle, rule, and heuristic have been observed as concerns—clarity of concept identification, completeness, and coherence of the concepts and their level of description, there are no grounds for assuming greater potential of the one over the other and importantly not principle or rule over heuristic.

REVIEW

The chapter characterises principles, rules and heuristics as potential or actual explicit and pre-scriptive HCI design knowledge, supporting design. It also describes and critiques their current state and identifies the associated challenge. Principles, rules, and heuristics constitute a form of HCI design knowledge. The latter is acquired and validated explicitly by case studies to solve the general HCI problem of design with the particular scope of humans interacting with computers to do something as desired, as viewed from a discipline perspective. The latter is espoused here for the development of HCI-EDPs. The chapter complements the preceding ones on design knowledge as craft artefacts and design practice experience and as HCI models and methods. It also contrasts with the following chapter on HCI-EDPs.

7.4   PRACTICE ASSIGNMENT

Describe the assumptions made by your research as concerns—principles (as in § 7.2.1), rules (as in § 7.2.2), and heuristics (as in § 7.2.3), as HCI design knowledge to support HCI design practice. If you have no research of your own at this time, select suitable research of a colleague or supervisor/instructor/teacher. Alternatively, select a suitable publication from the HCI research literature.

- Contrast the similarities and differences between the assumptions made by your (or that of other's) research and the proposals made here.

- How might the differences be made coherent? If they cannot be made coherent, why might this be so?

Select an interactive human-computer interface, either one described in the HCI research or professional design literature or one, of which you have practical experience. Also, select a single principle, rule or heuristic from each of those presented here.

- Apply each principle (see § 7.2.1), rule (see § 7.2.2), and heuristic (see § 7.2.3) to the interactive human-computer interface, chosen above.

- How well did you apply the principle, rule, and heuristic on a scale of 1 to 5?

- How easy or difficult was it to apply the principle, rule and heuristic on a scale of 1 to 5.

Select a different interactive human-computer interface and repeat the practice assignment.

• Note any similarities or differences between the two practice assignments.

• Why might this be so?

Guidelines[4] and standards[5] are also forms of HCI design knowledge.
Select two papers from the HCI research literature, one for each type of design knowledge.

• Are the examples more like principles (see § 7.2.1), rules (see§ 7.2.2), or heuristics (see § 7.2.3)? If so, try to identify the features, which make them different? If not, then characterise them in the terms of § 7.2.1–§ 7.2.3 as putative guidelines[4] and gtandards.[5]

• Repeat the previous practice assignment for guidelines and for standards.

Hints and Tips

Difficult to get started?

Try reading the chapter again, while at the same time thinking about how to describe your own (or that of others) HCI principles, rules, and heuristics, as HCI design knowledge. Note similarities and differences between the two lines of thought, as you go along.

• Describe your (or that of others) HCI principles, rules and heuristics, as HCI design knowledge, in its own terms, before attempting to apply those proposed here.

Difficult to complete?

Familiarise yourself with the main ways of conceptualising HCI principles, rules, and heuristics, as HCI design knowledge, identified in the HCI literature, before attempting to address those proposed here.

Test

List from memory as many of the section titles as you can.

7.5   NOTES

[1] It might be argued that principles proposed some time ago now by Wickens are no longer relevant to present HCI research thinking. The argument, however, is rejected.

First, additional Wickens publications have appeared, since the date of the original publication, for example, Wickens, Lee, and Becker (2004).

Second, Wickens principles-associated work is cited by more recent publications, for example, in the context of human factors in the design of air traffic control systems (Timmer and Long, 2002).

Third, it is unclear either what has replaced principles, other than rules and heuristics or how the latter have advanced the unknown validity, and so unreliable and ineffective, status of principles.

The same case, as for Wickens, can be made, concerning the principles of Norman. Additional more recent publications for the latter include—Norman (2010 and 2013).

[2] It might also be argued, as in the case of Wickens, that rules proposed some time ago now by Shneiderman are no longer relevant to present HCI research thinking. The argument, however, is rejected.

First, additional Shneiderman publications have appeared, since the date of the original publication, for example, Shneiderman and Plaisant (2004) and Shneiderman (2010).

Second, Shneiderman rules-associated work is cited by more recent publications, for example, Rogers et al. (2011) in the context of their textbook on interaction design.

Third, it is unclear either what has replaced rules, other than heuristics or how the latter have advanced the unknown validity and so unreliable and ineffective status of rules.

Last, it is interesting to note in passing, that the guidelines, used in the business-to-consumer electronic commerce case study of 2007 are those of Bidigare (2000), Chaparro (2001), Kienan (2001), and Walsh (2003). This indicates that guidelines were alive and well, at the time the HCI-EDP research was conducted and further suggests, that they continue to be so to this day.

[3] It might also be argued, as in the case of Wickens and Shneiderman, that heuristics proposed some time ago now by Nielsen are no longer relevant to present HCI research thinking. The argument, however, is rejected.

Nielsen-associated work is cited by more recent publications, for example, Rogers et al. (2011) in the context of their textbook on interaction design.

Third, it is unclear either what has replaced heuristics or how any such replacement has advanced the unknown validity and so unreliable and ineffective status of heuristics.

[4] Many different sorts of guidelines are to be found in the research literature. For readers having difficulty selecting among them, the following guidelines are suitably edited for use for the practice assignment.

1. Design Process and Evaluation.

    Only display useful content. Unnecessary content inhibits good performance. Get to know what the users want. Get information between exchanges with actual users.

2. Optimising the User Experience.

    Having pop-ups or other unsolicited windows is frustrating. Make the interface professional. Keep a consistent sequence of processes to increase user experience.

3.   Accessibility.

Make the interface accessible to all users. Section 504 of the Rehabilitation Act requires interactive systems to be accessible by people with disabilities. Use assistive technology. Provide text for all images, animations, maps, and other media.

4.   Hardware and Software.

Make the interface compatible with the most popular browsers like Internet Explorer, Google Chrome, Firefox, and Safari. Find out what fonts, text size, and other browser settings users prefer. Make 95% of the users happy, if you can.

5.   Home Page.

Make sure the homepage is easy to access. Include all the most important links on it. Consider what kind of and how much content to include.

6.   Page Layout.

Put important items in the top centre of the page. Any comparative information should be next to each other and so easy to see. Do not make users go back and forth between pages to compare information. Use a level of importance that goes from high to low.

7.   Navigation.

Make sure the back button works. Also, that the labels on the tabs are easy to understand. Ensure the reader knows where they are and where they are going. Use sitemaps to get help, if needed.

8.   Scrolling and Paging.

Avoid horizontal scrolling. Help fast scrolling by highlighting or increasing the size of important items. Use paging as an option. Also, use links to other pages. Create more pages that are shorter to eliminate scrolling.

9.   Headings, Titles, and Labels.

Make headings, titles, and labels descriptive. Make the words meaningful. Make the headings or labels unique. Use the correct hierarchy, for headings. Provide clear options. Highlight important headings visually.

10. Links.

    Make the links relevant to the information on the page. Repeat important links, as needed. Use text links rather than image links. Use pointing and clicking instead of the mouse. Label internal versus external links, using appropriate link lengths.

11. Text Appearance.

    Keep font formatting consistent across the interface. Black text on a plain background is easier to read than other combinations. Use consistent formats with text items like times, dates, telephone numbers, and addresses. Avoid using CAPS Lock. Use bold and italic sparingly to attract attention. Use 12 points or larger.

12. Lists.

    Use a clear heading or title. Place the most important items at the top. Never use 0 as a number. Capitalise the first letter of the first word on each line.

13. Screen-Based Controls (Widgets).

    Drop-down boxes, push buttons, and icons are widgets. Label them clearly. Use widgets sparingly. Minimise data entry. Use the same data entry method consistently. Place the cursor automatically in the first data field for easy use. Use at least two radio buttons.

14. Graphics, Images, and Multimedia.

    Maintain consistency. Use logo images. Label images descriptively to identify their purpose. Use images that do not take up the whole background.

15. Writing Web Content.

    Incorporate all the information users need. Use words and phrases familiar to users. Define anything that needs comprehension. Use the active voice. Write instructions in the affirmative.

16. Content Organisation.

    Ensure a good user experience and good usability. Create page headings that are clear. Display only necessary information. No repeats on every page. Put the most important material in the top, centre of the page.

17. Search.

    Include a search toolbar on each page. Ensure all the forms of a word or phrase can be found. Include hints that help users find what they need. Use templates to simplify the process.

18. Usability Testing.

    Test for the usability of the website to ensure it is efficient and successful. Use real subjects that do not have any ties to your organisation. Make the changes needed and then test the website again (and again.....).

[5] Standards are not easy to access for individuals, as opposed to organisations. Even for the latter, standards acquisition may involve some form of payment or commitment. For the purposes of the practice assignment, assume the following to be an example of standards. Complete the practice assignment as instructed.

Standards for interactive human-computer systems provide advice of the following kind.

1. Be consistent.

2. Offer informative feedback.

3. Ask for authentication of any critical action.

4. Authorise easy reversal of actions.

5. Lessen the information that needs to be remembered between actions.

6. Seek competence in dialogue, motion and thought.

7. Excuse mistakes.

8. Classify activities by function and establish screen geography accordingly.

9. Deliver help services that are context sensitive.

10. Use simple action verbs or short verb phrases to name commands.

PART III

HCI Engineering Design Principles: A Way Forward for HCI Design Knowledge

The third part of the book presents the conceptions of HCI engineering design principles required and applied in the acquisition of initial HCI-EDPs. The latter are intended to meet the challenge posed by the critique of HCI design knowledge of making the latter more reliable in its support for HCI design practice. This part summarises the two case studies reporting the acquisition of initial HCI-EDPs in the domains of domestic energy planning and control, and business-to-customer electronic commerce. This part also identifies the future research required to acquire further such HCI-EDPs.

CHAPTER 8

HCI Engineering Design Principles as a Way Forward for HCI Design Knowledge

SUMMARY

The chapter introduces principles, engineering principles, HCI principles, and HCI engineering design principles, such as design knowledge. HCI principles, as currently formulated, are distinguished from HCI-EDPs. HCI principles are exemplified. Some examples, as best-practice, are applied in the two case studies of HCI-EDP acquisition, summarised in Chapter 9 and reported in full in the companion volume (Long et al., 2022, in press). Other examples are not so used, but could be applied to acquire future HCI-EDPs. Also presented is a critique of HCI design knowledge, its current state and the associated challenge. HCI-EDPs constitute one form of explicit and prescriptive HCI design knowledge. They are acquired and can be validated by case studies solving the general HCI problem of design, the latter having the particular scope of humans interacting with computers to do something as desired. Both general question and particular scope are conceived from a discipline perspective. The introduction, as one type of HCI design knowledge, is preceded in the three previous chapters as craft artefacts and design practice experience, models and methods, and HCI principles, rules, and heuristics. The following chapter summarises two case studies of the acquisition of initial HCI-EDPs.

8.1 PRINCIPLES

In general, principles are considered to constitute a basic component of discipline knowledge at least for the disciplines of science and engineering. Depending on the discipline, principles may take the form of truth proposition, law, rule, model, prescription, method, doctrine, or theory. However, in all cases, principles serve as a goal for research as the acquisition and the validation of discipline knowledge. Principles, then, embody the purpose of discipline knowledge, which is to support discipline practice.

8.2   ENGINEERING PRINCIPLES

Engineering principles generally constitute a basic component of engineering discipline knowledge. Engineering principles may take the form of truth proposition, law, rule, model, doctrine, method, or theory, as they pertain to engineering. However, in all cases, engineering principles serve as a goal for engineering research as the acquisition and the validation of engineering knowledge. Engineering principles, then, embody the purpose of engineering knowledge, which is to support engineering practice. The latter may take the form of "trial and error," "specify, implement, and test," and "specify then implement," among others. Note that only the latter does not include or imply iteration of the design knowledge in its application, as opposed to in its acquisition. Iteration with respect to satisfying user and other requirements, however, is different.

Such engineering principles may or may not include scientific principles or elements thereof. Artefacts designed on the basis of engineering principles, include bridges, ships, and buildings. Engineering principles can be contrasted with scientific principles. The former are created to support design as the specification and implementation of artefacts. The latter are created to support understanding of natural phenomena as explanation and prediction.

8.3   HCI PRINCIPLES

Consistent with principles (see § 8.1), but more particularly, HCI principles constitute a basic component of HCI discipline knowledge (see also Long, 2021). This position accords with Cockton's view, that "principled knowledge is a mark of any established disciplinary practice" (Cockton, 2009). HCI principles may take the form of model, truth proposition, method, law, rule, doctrine, or theory, as they pertain to HCI. However, in all cases, HCI principles serve as a basis for HCI research as the acquisition and the validation of HCI knowledge from a discipline perspective. HCI principles, then, embody the purpose of HCI knowledge, which is to support HCI design practice. The latter may take the form of "trial and error," "specify, implement, and test," and "specify then implement," among others. Note that only the latter does not include or imply iteration of the HCI design knowledge. Iteration of design practice with respect to satisfying user and other requirements, however, is different.

Such HCI principles may or may not include scientific principles or elements thereof, such as cognitive models or experimental methods. HCI principles can be contrasted with scientific principles, such as those of cognitive psychology. The former are created to support HCI design as the specification and implementation of interactive human-computer systems to satisfy user and other requirements. The latter are created to support understanding as explanation and prediction of natural phenomena, which may also include users interacting with computers.

However, a review of the HCI research literature fails to identify any principles, which support design practice as "specify then implement" in the absence of iteration in its application. The failure, however, is not due to the absence of references to HCI principles (see § 7.2.1). It is rather due to the nature and state of the principles, proposed to date as HCI design knowledge.

8.4   HCI ENGINEERING DESIGN PRINCIPLES

Following the earlier definition of HCI principles (see § 8.3), HCI-EDPs constitute a basic component of HCI engineering discipline knowledge. HCI-EDPs serve as a basis for HCI engineering research as the acquisition and the validation of HCI engineering design knowledge. HCI-EDPs, then, embody the purpose of knowledge, which is to support HCI engineering design practice. The relationship is shown in Figure 8.1, which should be compared with Figures 1–7.1 for similarities and differences. Likewise, as a format for alternative conceptions, which readers might like to formulate for themselves.

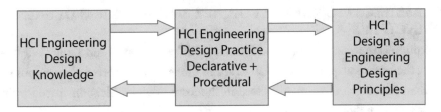

Figure 8.1: HCI design knowledge as HCI engineering design principles.

Such HCI-EDPs may or may not include scientific principles or elements thereof, such as cognitive models. HCI-EDPs can be contrasted with scientific principles, such as those of cognitive psychology. The former are created to support HCI design as the specification and implementation of interactive systems. The latter are created to support understanding of natural phenomena as explanation and prediction including, for example, understanding of humans interacting with computers.

However, a review of the HCI research literature fails to identify the existence of any HCI-EDPs supporting "specify then implement" design practice, as described above. As concerns HCI theory, the failure is simply for want of referencing HCI engineering in general. For example, following Rogers (2012), this is the case for cognition theories (extended, distributed, ecological), social theories (computer-supported co-operative work (CSCW), situated action), and other types of theory (ethnographic, grounded, design, human values, technology as experience, in-the-wild). None of these types of HCI theory appears to make specific reference to HCI engineering.

As concerns HCI frameworks, in contrast, HCI engineering is frequently referenced. For example, Card et al. (1983) make clear the relations that they consider to exist between HCI engineering and HCI design. Shneiderman (1998) identifies relationships between HCI and software engineering and conceives HCI design as engineering. Barnard (1991) makes reference to the possibility of principled design support provided by engineering tools, based on cognitive models, such as interacting cognitive subsystems. Rauterberg (2006) views both HCI design and development as engineering. Last, Carroll (2003 and 2010) considers HCI science to be the basis for engineering models, developed and applied by engineers and designers.

HCI-EDPs, in contrast, are but rarely referenced. Further, when referenced (Wickens et al., 2004; Norman, 2013; see also § 7.2.1), their status is little different from that of rules (see § 7.2.2) or heuristics (see § 7.2.3), rather than constituting the fundamental basis of HCI engineering discipline design knowledge, supporting design practice as "specify then implement." In addition, the references have little or nothing to say as concerns the required conceptualisation, not to mention the operationalisation, test, and generalisation, and so the validation, of such HCI-EDPs from a discipline perspective.

8.4.1   CLASSIFICATION SPACE FOR HCI ENGINEERING DESIGN PRINCIPLES

The one exception is the work of Long and Dowell (1989) and Dowell and Long (1989). Although they have not themselves acquired any HCI-EDPs in the research reported, they propose a detailed theoretical characterisation of them, expressed in the form of a classification space for design disciplines, which they apply to HCI. The latter is shown in Figure 8.2.

The classification space is bounded by "discipline practices," "discipline knowledge" (see also Figures 3.1 and 4.1), and "general design problems" (see also Figures 1.1 and 2.1).

Discipline practices lie on a dimension of "specification completeness," which goes from "soft problems," which are not specifiable (or only incompletely so) to design problems, which exhibit complete specification (at least for the purposes in hand). In terms of specification completeness, the design problems go from "implement and test" to "specify and implement" and to "specify then implement."

General design problems lie on a dimension of "determinism," which goes from "soft problems" to "hard problems."

Discipline knowledge lies on a dimension of "formality of knowledge," which goes from "experience" to "principles."

The classification is divided by the "boundary of determinism." The latter supports the location of contemporary HCI and a future possible engineering discipline of HCI. Contemporary HCI design knowledge solves essentially (but not exclusively) hard, that is well specified problems, with design practices, somewhere between "implement and test," supported by knowledge as "design experience," and "specify and implement" practice, supported by "informal' design knowledge."

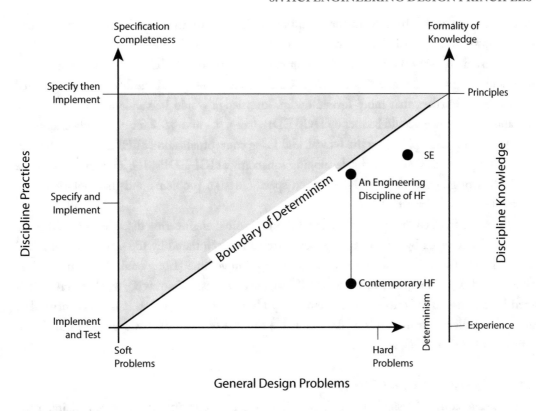

Figure 8.2: **A classification space for design disciplines (following Dowell and Long, 1989).**

Dowell and Long argue that the completeness of a discipline's specification of realised design solutions depends on the hardness of the general design problem. However, the actual completeness is determined by the formality of its knowledge. In the case of the HCI discipline, the latter ranges from the experience of designers to HCI-EDPs. Within the boundary of determinism, HCI-EDPs could be expressed as formal knowledge to support "specify then implement" design practice. The formal knowledge would comprise both declarative principles—the "what" of interactive system design and procedural principles, the "'how" of interactive system design.

A future possible engineering discipline of HCI, in contrast, would solve the same type of problems with design practices, somewhere between "specify and implement" and "'specify then implement," supported by more formal design knowledge, that is HCI-EDPs.

Dowell and Long's conceptualisation of HCI-EDPs does not identify their individual constituent concepts, other than by the context in which they appear. Further, the relations between concepts at the same and at different levels of description are not specified. Last, it claims to be neither complete nor coherent. In spite of these shortcomings, it is the only conceptualisation of HCI-EDPs, intended to support "specify then implement" design practice, to be found in the HCI research literature at this time (with the exception of design patterns—see § 8.4.2). It is also one that has constituted the basis for the research of others, including the present.[1]

For example, using the Dowell and Long conceptualisation of HCI-EDPs as a basis, Cummaford and Long (1998) argue that current HCI design knowledge is insufficiently well specified to be validated. Further, that more formal design knowledge would be validatable (Cummaford, 2000) and that this need could be met by HCI-EDPs (see § 9.1 and § 9.2 for case study examples).

As a further example, using the Dowell and Long conceptualisation of HCI-EDPs as a basis, Stork (1999) proposes a strategy for developing substantive HCI-EDPs. The strategy involves the identification of general relationships between specific design problems and their solutions (see § 9.1 for a case study example).

The move from contemporary HCI to a future possible engineering discipline of HCI is the way forward, envisaged by this book. The way forward is instantiated by the acquisition of initial HCI-EDPs, published in full elsewhere in the companion volume (Long et al., 2022, in press). A summary of this work appears in Chapter 9 to support the case of a way forward for HCI. It is offered in response to the critique of contemporary HCI design knowledge. It is a way forward to address the challenge facing HCI of the unreliable support of design knowledge for HCI design practice (see § 2–5.3, § 6.5, and § 7.3).

8.4.2   HCI DESIGN PATTERNS

It might be argued that "design patterns"[1] constitute another exception to the general claim, made above. The latter asserts, that references to principles have little or nothing to say as concerns the required conceptualisation, not to mention the evaluation and validation, of HCI-EDPs. This is in complete agreement with the critiques advanced in § 7.3. The design patterns argument makes a number of additional points, which warrant its more detailed presentation, which follows.

The concept of design patterns originates in architecture with Alexander (1979). He realised the need to identify generic solutions as a way of exploiting the re-use of architects' design experience. Such design solutions are intended to support the user-centred design of spaces, in which humans can live as desired.

Design patterns have gained some popularity in HCI, following a CHI'97 workshop, reported by Bayle et al.—*Towards a Pattern Language for Interaction Design* (1997). Bayle et al. define an interaction design pattern as one "that describes a connection between a repeatedly encountered problem and a solution that has been proven in the field, across time and circumstance." Gamma et al. (1995) and Seffah (2015) promote the development of design patterns in software engineering as a means of improving the re-usability of object-oriented software.

Such interaction design patterns are of interest here, because they appear to be embarking on the quest for more reliable HCI design, much as HCI-EDPs.[1] Interaction design patterns attempt to acquire HCI knowledge with:

1.   separation of problem from solution;

2.   focus on being proven in specific design;

3.   structure in the form of a standard template for pattern representation, express-ing-problem, force, solution, and comments; and

4.   strategy for their acquisition through "writers' workshop," a form of constructive peer criticism. There has also been consideration of software engineering patterns on the different merits of analysing past designs versus analysing current designs versus analysing designers' experience.

However, this knowledge lacks some of the requirements for HCI-EDPs as expressed by Dowell and Long (1989)—see also Figure 8.2. The missing requirements, as applied to interaction design patterns, are:

1.   complete and coherent conceptualisation of interaction design patterns (at least more rigorous than at present) from a discipline perspective;

2.   operationalisation of interactive design patterns for the purpose of evaluation, as a preliminary to validation;

3.   evaluation of the interaction design pattern to include—its generality and some expression of its performance with respect to the associated design problem and its solution; and

4.   validation of the interaction design pattern to include test and generalisation.

In conclusion, it is accepted that interaction design patterns are a potential response to the challenge of more reliable HCI design practice.[1] However, since the proposal for HCI-EDPs, as presented by Dowell and Long (1989), is more complete and coherent and so fit-for-purpose, from a discipline perspective, than for the interaction design patterns, then carrying forward the former is also considered to carry forward the latter for the purposes in hand.

8.5   STATE OF HCI ENGINEERING DESIGN PRINCIPLES

The concept of HCI-EDPs, as proposed in the previous section, forms the basis for considering their state, which follows. HCI-EDPs constitute the basis for an HCI engineering discipline. They embody its essential characteristics. HCI-EDPs are intended to support interactive system design effectively and as desired. The latter is effected by the specification and implementation of such systems. HCI-EDPs, once conceptualised, operationalised, tested, and generalised, and so validated, offer the assurance of the reliability of their application in HCI design practice, as specify then implement. HCI-EDP design knowledge supports the solution of design problems by specify then implement design practices.

As reported earlier, a search of the general HCI research literature fails to identify the existence of any such HCI-EDPs. Failure also results both from examination of HCI frameworks (Long, 2021) and HCI theories (Rogers, 2012). Further, these sources fail to identify the concept of HCI-EDPs, with one exception—that of Dowell and Long (1989).[1] This exception has already been described in some detail (see § 8.4). This conceptualisation is common to both case studies, reporting initial acquisition of such principles, summarised in § 9.1 and § 9.2 and also reported in full in the companion volume (Long et al., 2022, in press). The case studies, then, constitute the de facto current state of HCI-EDPs. Only their relationship with the Dowell and Long conception needs to be addressed and illustrated here.

Dowell and Long characterise the design disciplines by the "softness" or "hardness" of their general design problem. Soft and hard problems are differentiated by their "determinism for purpose," that is to say, by the requirement for design solutions to be determinate. The latter is instantiated by the first case study as the behaviours of users, as desired for domestic energy planning and control. Likewise, in the second case study, as the behaviours of users interacting with computers as desired for business-to-consumer electronic commerce. Both the specific planning and control domestic energy user behaviours and the specific business-to-consumer electronic commerce user behaviours are deterministic, for the purposes in hand. As concerns HCI, that purpose is their embodiment in HCI-EDPs. User behaviours in both domains are determined, at least within the limits required by a particular design solution, respectively, by domestic energy planning and control and electronic commerce transaction system protocols.

Dowell and Long claim that disciplines differ as to the completeness with which they specify solutions to their general design problem before implementation. Some disciplines specify solutions completely before implementation. Their practices may be characterised as "specify then implement," for example some practices of electrical engineering. Other disciplines do not specify their solutions before their implementation. Their practices may be characterised as "implement and test," for example, innovation design. Other disciplines specify solutions partially before their implementation, for example, software engineering. Their practices may be characterised as "specify and implement." Both the domestic energy planning and control and the business-to-consumer electronic commerce case studies' specific design problems and associated design solutions are intended to be complete, such that any acquired and validated HCI-EDPs would support "specify then implement" HCI design practice, within the scope of the principles.

8.6   HCI ENGINEERING DESIGN PRINCIPLE AS A WAY FORWARD FOR HCI DESIGN KNOWLEDGE

The effectiveness of HCI design knowledge to support HCI design practice is identified earlier as a challenge to HCI design knowledge generally and to HCI principles, in particular (see § 3.5). HCI-EDPs are proposed here as a form of design knowledge to meet this challenge. The latter can be met in two ways. First, empirical validation of the design knowledge as HCI-EDPs, once acquired. Second, analytic instance/class embodiment of the generalisation of the design problems and solutions, used to acquire the design knowledge as HCI-EDPs. Both ways are intended to assure the effectiveness of HCI engineering knowledge for design practice.

Empirical validation is the first way of assuring the effectiveness of HCI engineering design principles. More generally and following Long (2010 and 2021), empirical validation of such HCI design knowledge, requires conceptualisation, which is complete, coherent, and fit-for-purpose for operationalisation, which is complete, coherent, and fit-for-purpose for test, which is complete, coherent and fit-for-purpose for generalisation, which, taken together, is complete, coherent and fit-for-purpose for validation, as viewed from a discipline perspective. Validation can be conducted and reported in terms of case studies, with a view to establishing the current state of the effectiveness of the HCI-EDPs of interest.

HCI research in general has always recognised the need for empirical validation. For example, John and Gray (1995), Atwood, Gray, and John (1996), and Teo and John (2008) all report case studies intended to validate the models of Card et al. (1983). Elsewhere, Long and Monk (2002) report a case study, in which a framework for HCI as engineering is applied analytically to an instance of telemedical consultation research (Watts and Monk, 1997 and 1998) to establish how the former might inform the latter. Long and Brostoff (2002) report research intended to validate HCI design knowledge, in the form of the products of a structured analysis and design Method for USability Engineering (MUSE—Lim and Long, 1994). Last, Long and Hill (2005) report research, which aims to validate design knowledge, proposed by Timmer and Long (2002) for air traffic management. The design knowledge is expressed as a theory of the operator planning horizon (TOPH). The challenge for HCI-EDPs is first to ensure that the principles are validatable. In addition, to ensure their validation is effected.

As concerns the second way of assuring the effectiveness of HCI engineering design knowledge, Cummaford and Long (1998) propose to embed principle generalisation in the acquisition process of the principle itself. Generalisation is the final stage of the empirical validation process, proposed by Dowell and Long. Later, for example, Cummaford and Long propose the class-first creation of HCI-EDPs, which are general to classes of HCI design solutions to classes of HCI design problems (as summarised in § 9.2).

Stork (1999) similarly proposes an instance-first strategy for developing HCI-EDPs, which requires research to identify general relationships between specific design problems and their solutions. This identification of general relationships in turn requires the operationalisation of specific HCI design problems and their solutions from the conceptions of specific HCI design problems and specific HCI design solutions (as summarised in § 9.1).

Last, Cummaford (2007) proposes that the specification of problems and solutions, at the level of classes, is required for HCI-EDP acquisition. Further, to develop such principles, iterative identification is necessary of class design problems and their class design solutions. The commonalities both between them and between the commonalities themselves form the basis for an HCI-EDP. The latter would then apply to all HCI-EDPs within its scope. Such formal (that is completely specified) HCI-EDPs would offer the possibility to "specify then implement" design solutions to "hard" (determinate) design problems (see § 8.4).

These different ways of meeting the challenge of acquiring engineering design principles for HCI as design knowledge are further developed in the case studies of initial HCI-EDP acquisition, presented in the following chapter.

REVIEW

The chapter introduces HCI-EDPs as a basic component of HCI design knowledge. The state of HCI-EDPs, is described, assessed, and exemplified. The challenge of ensuring the effectiveness of HCI-EDP support for "specify then implement" design is identified and illustrated. Acquisition and validation of principles are evaluated as to their potential contribution to the assurance of design support effectiveness. The introduction to HCI-EDPs constitutes the basis for the following chapter, which presents two case studies summarising the acquisition of initial such HCI-EDPs[4].

8.7   PRACTICE ASSIGNMENT

For the sake of completeness and for the purposes in hand, two additional major examples of HCI design knowledge are identified here in addition to those presented in § 7.2 and which are referenced in § 7.4. These forms of HCI knowledge are guidelines[2] and standards.[3] It might be assumed that these forms of knowledge can be contrasted with HCI-EDPs in the manner of principles, rules and heuristics with the same conclusion. However, no detailed consideration is offered here in the manner of that presented in the case of the latter. Detailed consideration involves the three criteria of clarity of definition, completeness, and coherence.

Search the HCI research literature for examples of guideleines[2] and standards.[3] Select one of each. Submit each to consideration of clarity of definition, completeness, and coherence with respect to the same criteria applied to HCI-EDPs. Follow the same assessment process as applied in § 7.2 for principles, rules, and heuristics.

- What conclusions result from your assessment?

- If different from those of § 7.2 try to rationalise why this might be so.

Identify from the HCI research literature one or more types of HCI discipline knowledge, additional to those of guidelines and standards (and also to principles, rules, and heuristics), for example interaction design patterns (see § 8.4).

Repeat the same assessment as conducted for guidelines and standards.

- Contrast your findings with the specification of HCI-EDPs, offered in § 8.4. The aim of the practice assignment is to encourage readers to think and to reason about the different types of design knowledge, such that they can apply and acquire them more easily and appropriately.

Hints and Tips

Difficult to get started?

Try reading § 8.3 again, while at the same time thinking about the forms of HCI design knowledge with which you are familiar. Note similarities and differences between the two lines of thought, as you go along.

Describe the forms of HCI design knowledge in their own terms, before attempting to apply those proposed here.

Difficult to complete?

Familiarise yourself with the major forms of HCI design knowledge, identified in the HCI literature, before attempting to address those of guidelines and standards.

Test

List from memory as many of the section titles as you can.

8.8   NOTES

[1] It is unclear how interaction design patterns relate to the problem hardness of general design problems and the specification completeness of discipline practices (Dowell and Long, 1989). Also, within the boundary of determinism, how the formality of the knowledge is expressed in interaction design patterns, to support what kind of design practice. Last, it is unclear whether interaction design principles would be validatable in the manner claimed for HCI-EDPs.

[2] See 7.5 Note [4].

[3] See 7.5 Note [5].

[4] As a personal communication, it is interesting to note an insightful comment made by an anonymous reviewer—"Based on participating in a U.S. National Research Council report (Pew

and Mavor, 2007), I ended up seeing HCI as being really two fields. In one field, practitioners (and researchers helping them) want to know about design. This group is skewed towards industry, but not exclusively. I think the Long et al. book is in this group. This area has not been as studied in HCI, but is a major area, and has often been overlooked by the field because it is harder to do, more applied, and harder to publish. Yet, even major researchers in the next group rely on its results to design their own systems. In the other, closely allied and often confused group with them, is researchers interested in usability in a singular environment, or a single HCI method. This group skews towards academics, almost exclusively."

CHAPTER   9

Case Studies of the Acquisition of Initial HCI Engineering Design Principles

SUMMARY

The two case studies of the acquisition of initial HCI-EDPs, as a way forward for HCI design knowledge, concern the domains of domestic energy planning and control and business-to-consumer electronic commerce. Each case study is summarised here in sufficient detail to support the claim of HCI-EDPs to be one possible way forward for HCI design knowledge. The final chapter assesses the claim. It also identifies the research required to make the initial HCI-EDPs final and to acquire additional, future such principles.

9.1   DOMESTIC ENERGY PLANNING AND CONTROL CASE STUDY

The case study comprises an introduction to domestic energy planning and control EDPs, two development cycles for their acquisition, their presentation, and an assessment and discussion of their state. Full publication of the case studies appears elsewhere in the companion volume (Long et al. 2022, in press).

9.1.1   INTRODUCTION TO HCI ENGINEERING DESIGN PRINCIPLES

The section begins with a conception of substantive EDPs, which espouses the Dowell and Long (1989) conception of the general design problem of the discipline of HCI (Long and Dowell, 1989).[1] Both design problem and discipline conceptions distinguish the domain of application and the interactive worksystem. The relationship is one of "effects/monitors." The latter comprises human(s) and computer(s). The relationship is one of "interacts." The behavioural system and work distinction is shown in Figure 9.1.

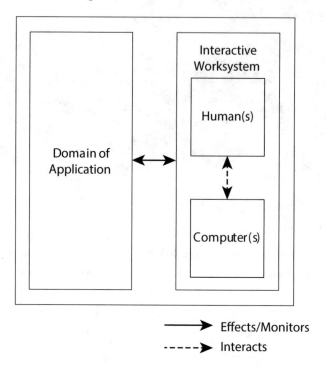

Figure 9.1: Behavioural system and work distinction (following Stork, 1999).

The section continues with a conception of declarative HCI-EDPs, conceptions of the general design problem and solution, conceptions of the specific design problem and solution, a review of the conception of declarative EDPs, and an informal assessment of the conception of Dowell and Long (1989).

In turn, the conceptions of the general design problem and solution include conceptions of actual performance, desired quality, actual quality, desired costs and actual costs. Also, included is a conception of the HCI engineering practice, as shown in Figure 9.2.

There follows a strategy for developing HCI-EDPs, which comprises the strategy itself, a comparison with other strategies, scoping the research using the potential for planning and control EDPs, acquiring potential guarantee, shorter-term research benefits, overview of MUSE (Method for USability Engineering—Lim and Long, 1994) and the development cycle user requirements selection criteria. The latter include Cycle 1 selection, which in turn includes identified user requirements and comparison against the criteria and Cycle 2 criteria, which likewise include identified user requirements and comparison against criteria.

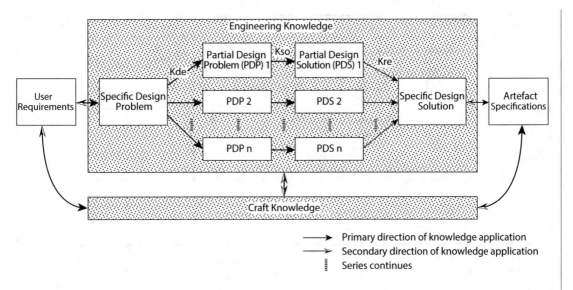

Figure 9.2: HCI engineering practice (following Stork, 1999).

Then follows a conception of human-computer systems, which comprises interactive worksystem costs, potential human cognitive structures, potential human physical structures (Human Architecture—see Figure 9.3), potential computer abstract structures, and potential computer physical structures (Computer Architecture—see Figure 9.4).

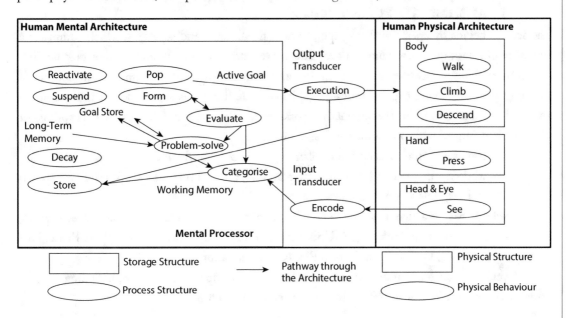

Figure 9.3: Human architecture (following Stork, 1999).

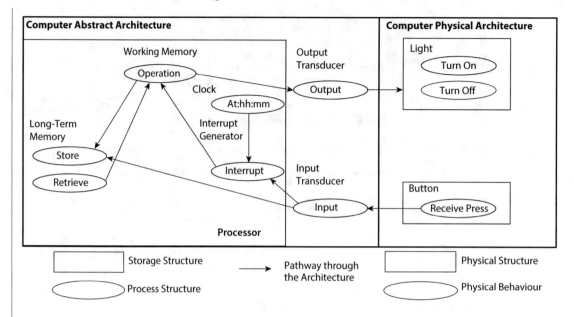

Figure 9.4: Computer architecture (following Stork, 1999).

9.1.2   DEVELOPMENT CYCLE 1 FOR THE ACQUISITION OF HCI ENGINEERING DESIGN PRINCIPLES FOR DOMESTIC ENERGY PLANNING AND CONTROL

The section begins by operationalising specific design problems and solutions, which comprises a framework for task quality, a framework for interactive worksystem costs, and composite structures.

There follows a conception of planning and control. The latter comprises conceptions of planning and control with claims for design guidance, including plans, assumed to be in the domain and plans, assumed to be in the interactive worksystem. The latter is followed by conceptions of planning and control with no claims for design guidance.

Then comes an initial conception of planning and control, which comprises control domain and control worksystem, planning worksysyem, plan domain, and planning worksystem (as shown in Figure 9.5). Last, follows operationalisation.

Cycle 1 best-practice development comprises user requirements, artefact specification, best-practice development, including MUSE design Information Elicitation Analysis Phase, Design Synthesis Phase, Design Specification Phase, and evaluation.

Cycle 1 operationalisation comprises current solution operationalisation, including specific actual performance, specific actual quality and specific actual costs.

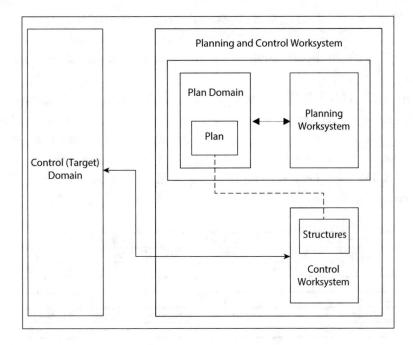

Figure 9.5: Conception of planning and control (following Stork, 1999).

Specific design problem operationalisation comprises specific desired quality and specific desired costs.

Specific design solution operationalisation comprises specific actual performance, specific actual quality, and specific actual costs.

9.1.3   DEVELOPMENT CYCLE 2 FOR THE ACQUISITION OF HCI ENGINEERING DESIGN PRINCIPLES FOR DOMESTIC ENERGY PLANNING AND CONTROL

The section begins with Cycle 2 best-practice development, which comprises user requirements, artefact specification, and best-practice development. The latter includes the MUSE design Information Elicitation and Analysis Phase, Design Synthesis Phase, and Design Specification Phase and evaluation.

There follows Cycle 2 operationalisation, including generality concerns, current solution operationalisation as specific actual performance, specific actual quality, and specific actual costs.

Next, comes specific design problem operationalisation, including specific desired quality and specific desired costs.

Last, specific design solution operationalisation comprises specific actual performance, specific actual quality, and specific actual costs.

9.1.4   PRESENTATION OF HCI ENGINEERING DESIGN PRINCIPLES FOR DOMESTIC ENERGY PLANNING AND CONTROL

The section begins with the detailed strategy, which comprises generality of the initial HCI-EDPs and generalisation over types,

Here is an initial HCI-EDP and its associated basis, identified during operationalisation.

The first example concerns the effort required by planning with respect to the benefits.

"Planning takes longer overall, is more effort overall, but provides the benefits. If the planning effort equates to the structural and behavioural costs in planning, then the operationalisations can be compared. The actual time taken for planning could be used, but would be difficult to measure. So the event ticks are used, which is the same as the behavioural costs."

Op1 Planning

Current structs		Actual structs		Difference	
Abstract	Physical	Abstract	Physical	Abstract	Physical
82	1	63	1	-19	0

Current behs		Actual behs		Difference	
Abstract		Abstract	Physical	Abstract	Physical
66	1	50	1	-16	0

Op2 Planning

Current structs		Actual structs		Difference	
Abstract	Physical	Abstract	Physical	Abstract	Physical
91	2	163	9	72	7

Current behs		Actual behs		Difference	
Abstract	Physical	Abstract	Physical	Abstract	Physical
214	5	1267	86	1053	81

The second example concerns an initial HCI-EDP, identified during operationalisation.

In the current system, StMonA is always followed directly by StSubPlanA, where the formulae show this outcome as, for example:

F11	A:StMonA:FP, FeelTemp, Temp, Comfort	
G11	A:StSubPlanA:RP, In house, Comfort	=F10

This situation is common to many of the formulae. This initial HCI-EDP can be shown in a notation:

$$A : StMonA : X, Y, Z \xrightarrow{1, e=1} A : StSubPlanA : P, Q, R$$

where, X, Y, Z and P, Q, R are parameters; the horizontal arrow shows the "followed by" relationship; the first equation under the arrow (1) shows the likelihood (probability) of the follow relationship, in this case one event tick; and the second equation under the arrow (*e*=1) shows the number of event ticks in the followed by relationship, in this case one event tick. In this HCI-EDP example, the solution concepts are null.

This initial HCI-EDP can be expressed in words as "Within Development Cycle 1, in the problem component, the Type A standard monitoring is always followed after one event tick by Type A standard sub-monitoring."

Next in the section comes an initial assumption assessment from operationalisation(s), including examples.

Likewise, inspirational initial HCI-EDPs from operationalisation are presented, including examples.

Last, are presented initial HCI-EDPs from general guidelines and from MUSE guidelines.

9.1.5   ASSESSMENT AND DISCUSSION OF HCI ENGINEERING DESIGN PRINCIPLES FOR DOMESTIC ENERGY PLANNING AND CONTROL

The section begins with assessment and discussion of the development strategy, including possible modifications to the strategy and the conception, status of initial HCI-EDPs, strategy assessment, further research and further strategy discussion.

There follows MUSE for research (MUSE/R), including scope and notation, process, support for design, and further research.

This completes the domestic energy planning and control case study summary.

9.2   BUSINESS-TO-CONSUMER ELECTRONIC COMMERCE CASE STUDY

The case study comprises an introduction to business-to-consumer electronic commerce HCI-EDPs, two development cycles for their acquisition, their presentation, and an assessment and discussion of their state.

9.2.1   INTRODUCTION TO HCI ENGINEERING DESIGN PRINCIPLES

The section begins with a conception of HCI-EDPs. The section comprises an introduction, a conception of the general design problem, a conception of the general design solution and a conception of the general HCI-EDP. The latter includes the scope of the general engineering design problem, declarative and procedural components of the general HCI-EDP, a summary of the general HCI-EDP and validation and ascription of guarantees to the HCI general EDP.

The strategy for HCI-EDP development follows, comprising introduction, including instance-first and class-first strategies, HCI-EDPs as class design knowledge, class development, definition of classes, conception of classes of design problem, conception of classes of design solution, and identification of promising classes.

Next, follows a method for the operationalising of the "class-first" strategy, comprising introduction, class design problem, and class design solution specification method, including the following.

Stage 1—Specify specific design problems.

Stage 2—Specify class design problem.

Stage 3—Evaluate class design problem.

Stage 4—Specify class design solution.

Stage 5—Specify specific design solutions.

Stage 6—Evaluate class design solution.

The method for class design problem and class design solution specification is shown in Figure 9.6.

There follows the HCI-EDP specification method.

Stage 1—Define HCI-EDP scope.

Stage 2—Define prescriptive design knowledge.

Stage 2.1— Identify class solution-only components.

Stage 2.2—Identify class design problem-only components.

Stage 2.3—Synthesise HCI-EDP prescriptive component.

Stage 3—Define HCI-EDP achievable performance.

Next, appears identification of class design problems, comprising introduction, and selection of potential class design problem, including work communalities, constituted of mercantile models (see Figure 9.7), transactions of the latter, followed by worksystem communalities.

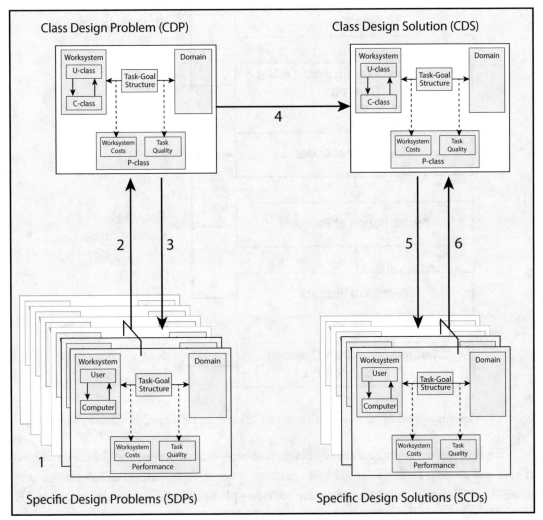

Figure 9.6: Method for class design problem and class design solution specification (following Cummaford, 2007).

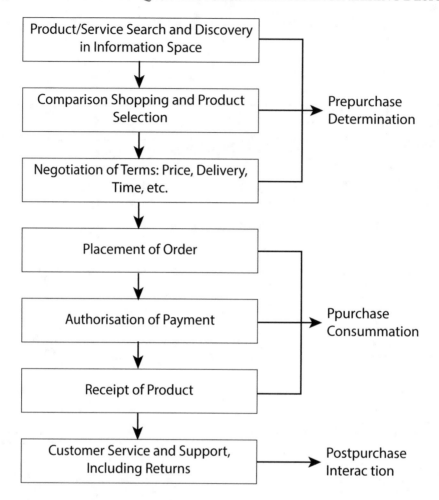

Figure 9.7: Mercantile model (following Kalakota and Whinston, 1996 cited by Cummaford, 2007).

The next section introduces class of design problem—transaction systems, made up of product goal and domain model, followed by transaction systems—specification of sub-classes, comprising class of design problem for transaction systems—physical goods, class of design problem for transaction systems—information, and assessment of subclasses.

9.2.2   DEVELOPMENT CYCLE 1 FOR THE ACQUISITION OF HCI ENGINEERING DESIGN PRINCIPLES FOR BUSINESS-TO-CONSUMER ELECTRONIC COMMERCE

The section begins with Cycle 1 development, comprising introduction, selection of systems for specific design problem and specific design solution development, testing procedure, including set up, participants, procedure, the testing tasks, and the calculation of user costs.

There follows the specification of specific design problems, including specific design problem 1a and specific design problem 1b.

Then specification of class design problem, followed by evaluation of class design problem, and specification of class design solution, specification of specific design solutions, including testing results. Last, follows evaluation of class design problem, specification of class design solution, and specification of specific design solutions, including testing results. Last evaluation of class design solution.

There follows Cycle 1 class design problem/class design solution specification and introduction, followed by:

> Stage 1—Specify specific design problems, including specific design problem 1a and specific design problem 1b.
>
> Stage 2—Specify class design problem, including domain and product goal, class worksystem, category mapping between models, task-goal structure, and performance.
>
> Stage 3—Evaluate class design problem.
>
> Stage 4—Specify class design solution, including domain and product goal and class worksystem.
>
> Stage 5—Specify specific design solutions.
>
> Stage 6—Evaluate class design solution, including actual performance.

9.2.3 DEVELOPMENT CYCLE 2 FOR THE ACQUISITION OF HCI ENGINEERING DESIGN PRINCIPLES FOR BUSINESS-TO-CONSUMER ELECTRONIC COMMERCE

The section begins with Cycle 2 development, including introduction, selection of systems for specific design problem, and specific design solution development, testing procedure, specification of specific design problems, specification of class design problem, evaluation of class design problem, specification of class design solution, specification of specific design solutions, and evaluation of class design solution.

Next comes Cycle 2 class design problem/class design solution specification, comprising introduction and method:

> Stage 1—Specify specific design problems.
>
> Stage 2—Specify class design problem.
>
> Stage 3—Evaluate class design problem.
>
> Stage 4—Specify class design solution.

Stage 5—Specify specific design solutions.

Stage 6—Evaluate class design solution.

9.2.4 PRESENTATION OF HCI ENGINEERING DESIGN PRINCIPLES FOR BUSINESS-TO-CONSUMER ELECTRONIC COMMERCE

The section begins with HCI-EDP specification, HCI-EDP scope, including requirement and instantiation. For examples from the latter, see Table 9.1 and Figure 9.8.

Table 9.1: HCI engineering design principle 1 - user representation structure states matrix (following Cummaford, 2007)

	Start	After T1	After T2	After T3	After T4	After T5	After T6	After T7
Abstract Structures								
Shopping knowledge	Starting state	Plus T1 increment	Plus T2 increment	Plus T3 increment	Plus T4 increment	Plus T5 increment	Plus T6 increment	Plus T7 increment
Payment knowledge	Starting state							Plus T7 increment
Value for money knowledge	Starting state	Plus T1 increment	Plus T2 increment	Plus T3 increment	Plus T4 increment	Plus T5 increment	Plus T6 increment	Plus T7 increment
Personal wherewithal knowledge	Starting state							Plus T7 increment
Plan for shopping								
Items to purchase	P1, P2, 2xP3	P2, 2xP3	2xP3		Minus 1xP3			
Items in order		P1	P1, P2	P1, P2, 2xP3	P1, P2, 2xP3	P1, P2, 1xP3	P1, P2, 1xP3	
Items subtotal	£0	P1cost	P1cost + P2cost	P1cost + P2cost + 2xP3cost	P1cost + P2cost + 2xP3cost	P1cost + P2cost + P3cost	P1cost + P2cost + P3cost	P1cost + P2cost + P3cost
Items purchased								P1, P2, 1xP3

There follows HCI-EDP prescriptive design knowledge, including identification of class design solution-only and class design problem-only components, identification of class design solution-only and class design problem-only abstract structures, comprising user representation structure states, computer representation structure states and identification of class design solution-only and class design problem-only physical structures.

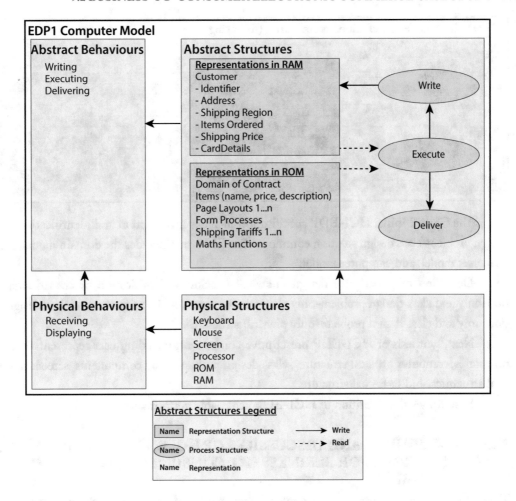

Figure 9.8: Engineering design principle 1—computer model (following Cummaford, 2007).

Next, comes user representation structure states, computer representation structure states, computer physical structures, including class design solution-only components and class design problem-only components, followed by screens and task-goal structures.

The section finishes with HCI-EDP achievable performance, see Table 9.2.

Table 9.2: Class design solution1 costs matrix (following Cummaford, 2007)

CDS1 (SDS1a + SDS1b)/2

		T1	T2	T3	T4	T5	T6	T7	Totals
Abstract behaviours	Plan	5	3	3	2	4	2	3	22
	Control	4	5	5	0	3	0	12	29
	Encode	4	2	3	1	3	1	5	19
	Execute	2	2	2	0	2	0	10	18
	Total	15	12	13	3	12	3	30	88
Physical behaviours	Search	3	2	3	0	3	0	5	16
	Click	3	3	3	0	2	0	27	38
	Keystroke	0	10	0	0	0	0	107	115
	Total	6	13	6	0	5	0	139	169
Task completion	Percentage	100.0%	100.0%	100.0%	100.0%	100.0%	100.0%	100.0%	100.0%
Time to complete (secs)	Average	10.5	16.333	20.083	19.583	13.583	5.0833	57.417	142.583333

The Cycle 2 initial HCI-EDP specification includes introduction and identification of class design problem/class design solution commonalities. The latter includes the domain model, product goal, user model, and computer model.

Definition of prescriptive design knowledge includes identification of class design solution-only and class design problem-only abstract structures and identification of class design solution-only and class design problem-only physical structures.

Next, synthesis of HCI-EDP prescriptive component, including user representation structure states, computer physical structures, class design problem-only components, screens and task-goal structures, and task-goal structure.

Last, comes the definition of HCI-EDP achievable performance.

9.2.5 ASSESSMENT AND DISCUSSION OF HCI ENGINEERING DESIGN PRINCIPLES FOR BUSINESS-TO-CONSUMER ELECTRONIC COMMERCE

The section begins with introduction, strategy assessment, and discussion, including specific design problems specification, comprising systems for specific design problem development selection, task selection, specific design problem prototypes, empirical testing and model selection, development, and specification.

Next, comes class design problem specification, class design problem evaluation, class design solution specification, specific design problem specification, class design solution evaluation, class design problem to class design solution mapping, HCI-EDP definition method, initial HCI-EDPs, requirements for validation, leading to guarantee review, HCI conceptions review and HCI-EDP.

This completes the business-to-customer electronic case study.

REVIEW

The chapter reports the summary of two case studies of the acquisition of initial HCI-EDPs. As the way forward for HCI design knowledge, the HCI-EDPs concern the domains of domestic energy planning and control and business-to-consumer electronic commerce. Each case study comprises an introduction to HCI-EDPs, two development cycles for the acquisition of such initial design principles, their presentation and an assessment and discussion, concerning HCI-EDPs.

9.3 PRACTICE ASSIGNMENT

9.3.1 GENERAL

Select a way forward for HCI design knowledge other than HCI-EDPs from craft artefacts and design practice experience (see Chapter 5), models and methods (see Chapter 6) or principles, rules, and heuristics (see Chapter 7). Select a domain other than domestic energy planning and control and business-to-customer electronic commerce.

- Sketch out with titles a case study, concerning the selected HCI design knowledge and the selected domain, comprising the following sections—introduction, two development cycles, design knowledge presentation and assessment, and discussion in the manner of 9.1/1–5 and 9.2/1–5.

- If you feel able to add any details to the titles, however limited, do so. The practice assignment is to get you to think about case studies, concerning the advancement of HCI design knowledge of whatever sort.

Hints and Tips

Difficult to get started?

Re-read the practice assignment task carefully.

- Make written notes and in particular list the sections, while re-reading 9.1/1–5 and 9.2/1-5.

- Think about how the sections might be applied to formulating your own assessment and discussion of the type of design knowledge for the case study of the selected domain.

- Re-attempt the practice assignment.

Test

List from memory as many of the section titles as you can.

9.3.2 PRACTICE SCENARIOS

Practice Scenario 9.1

Select a way forward for HCI design knowledge other than HCI-EDPs, craft artefacts and design practice experience (see Chapter 5), models and methods (see Chapter 6) or principles, rules and heuristics (see Chapter 7). Select a domain other than domestic energy planning, control and business-to-customer electronic commerce and the domain selected in § 9.3.1. Design guidelines or standards, as a form of HCI design knowledge would be acceptable. Also, other forms of HCI design knowledge.

- Sketch out with titles a case study, concerning the selected HCI design knowledge and the selected domain, comprising the following sections—introduction, two development cycles, design knowledge presentation and assessment, and discussion in the manner of 9.1/1–5 and 9.2/1–5.

- If you feel able to add any details to the titles, however limited, do so. The practice assignment is to get you to think about case studies, concerning the advancement of HCI design knowledge of whatever sort.

Test

List from memory as many of the section titles as you can.

Practice Scenario 9.2

Select a paper from the HCI research literature, which reports a case study of the acquisition of HCI design knowledge of whatever sort and concerning whatever domain.

- List the section titles, used to report the case study.

- Compare the titles with those listed in § 9.1–2 for completeness, coherence, and fitness-for- purpose. Note the main similarities and differences. Why might they be so?

Test

List from memory as many of the sections as you can.

9.4 NOTES

[1] Other associated references include—Smith et al. (1997); Dowell, (1998); Timmer and Long, (2002), and Hill (2010).

CHAPTER   10

Engineering Design Principles for HCI as a Way Forward for HCI Design Knowledge

SUMMARY

The chapter offers some ideas on how HCI design knowledge, in the form of craft artefacts and design practice experience, of models and methods, and of principles, rules, and heuristics might meet the challenge of more effective support for HCI design practice. However, the primary aim is to summarise progress and the associated carry forward, which claims to have been made towards the acquisition of HCI-EDPs. The common, and so general, progress is shared by the two case studies of domestic energy planning and control and of business-to-consumer electronic commerce, summarised in the previous chapter and reported in full in the companion volume (Long et al., 2022, in press). Further research to acquire and to validate HCI-EDPs is also identified.

10.1   TOWARD MORE EFFECTIVE DESIGN KNOWLEDGE TO SUPPORT HCI DESIGN PRACTICE

This book offers a critique of HCI design knowledge in general and in particular of craft artefacts and design practice experience (Chapter 5), models and methods (Chapter 6), and principles, rules, and heuristics (Chapter 7). The critique's primary contention is that such HCI design knowledge does not provide effective support for HCI design practice and may be only as good as the designer who is applying it.

Note that the book does not claim that such design knowledge is not of use to designers. Just that its effectiveness in this respect has too often not been demonstrated and so is not known explicitly. Neither does the book claim that HCI-EDPs are the only way forward for HCI design knowledge. Simply that it is one way forward and the way proposed here.

It could be asked, then, whether other forms of HCI design knowledge might also have their own ways forward? The answer is positive. However, this is not the book to make their case. That is for others and elsewhere (Hevner et al., 2004; Wickens et al., 2004; Norman, 2013; Roedl and Stolterman, 2013; Baxter et al., 2014; Da Silva et al., 2015). However, some ideas on the ways forward of HCI design knowledge, other than HCI-EDPs, follow. The aim is to illustrate the possibility and to allow readers to compare the other ways forward with that proposed for HCI-EDPs.

10.1.1 CRAFT ARTEFACTS AND DESIGN PRACTICE EXPERIENCE WAYS FORWARD FOR HCI DESIGN KNOWLEDGE

A general way forward for craft artefacts and design practice experience design knowledge would be to make it explicit and so more generally communicable. This way forward has been promoted extensively by Carroll (2003 and 2010). He presents "design rationale," as a theory, which supports the detailed representation of the history and meaning of an artefact. The interpretation is then synthesised as the knowledge implicit in the designs. The latter can then be applied explicitly in subsequent designs.

There exist other ways of making the implicit design knowledge of craft artefacts and design practice experience explicit and so more generally communicable. Designers themselves are able to describe and to explain informally the knowledge required for an artefact to be as it is and to function as it does. The knowledge may be incomplete and at varying levels of description, but other designers may still be able to make use of it.

Artefact producers can make better use of user feedback to support their design knowledge base. The feedback itself can be made more informative and more related to design and to designer's needs and understanding. Artefact acquirers can provide better diagnoses of product withdrawals and loss-making products, inspite of their competitive commercial concerns.

As to design practice, designers and their companies could be more open and communicative about their design processes, again inspite of competitive and market pressures.

10.1.2 MODELS AND METHODS WAYS FORWARD FOR HCI DESIGN KNOWLEDGE

A general way forward for models and methods design knowledge would be to improve their completeness, coherence, and fitness-for-purpose (and/or other relevant criteria).

Completeness with respect to the range and type of model could be improved, for example, by inclusion of domain models as well as human and computer models in the manner of Dowell (1998) and Hill (2010). Coherence, as concerns the level of detail of the models could be improved, for example, by frameworks specifying the required levels of description of the concepts and the relations between them, in the manner proposed by Long (2021). Fitness-for-purpose could be improved by the models suitability for design application and the empirical testing of models and their associated claims(Long and Hill, 2005).

Completeness with respect to the range and type of method could also be improved, for example, by the inclusion of all phases of the design process—from user requirements to interface design as proposed by Lim and Long (1994). Coherence, as concerns the specificity of guidance, could also be improved by relating their levels of description (for example, as in the case of Carroll, 2003 and 2010). Fitness of purpose could also be improved, as with models, by application of the methods to design and by the empirical testing of their associated claims.

10.1.3 PRINCIPLES, RULES AND HEURISTICS WAYS FORWARD FOR HCI DESIGN KNOWLEDGE

A general way forward for principles, rules, and heuristics design knowledge would be to improve their completeness, coherence and fitness-for-purpose (and/or other relevant criteria).

Completeness could be improved by their better specification, for example, including all aspects of "users interacting with computers to something as desired" (see Long, 2021). Coherence could be improved, for example, by their better specification of the relations between the concepts at the different levels of description. Their fitness-for-purpose could be improved by their suitability for design practice and by the empirical testing of their associated claims in case studies.

10.2 RESEARCH TOWARD ENGINEERING DESIGN PRINCIPLES FOR HCI

Both case studies claim to have made progress towards HCI-EDPs, a claim more fully supported in the companion volume (see Long et al., 2022, in press). These claims are referenced here for both the application domains of domestic energy planning and control (see § 9.1) and for business-to-consumer electronic commerce (see § 9.2). The claims, common to both case studies, are identified. The claims, then, can be considered general, at least with respect to the two case studies and their associated domains. They are cited here as part of the case that HCI-EDPs are one way forward for HCI design knowledge to meet the challenge of more reliable and so effective support for design practice.

10.2.1 RESEARCH PROGRESS TOWARD HCI ENGINEERING DESIGN PRINCIPLES

The claims that follow are common, and so general, to the two case studies in the application domains of domestic energy planning and control and of business-to-consumer electronic commerce.

1. Conception of HCI-EDPs (of some type).

2. Conceptions of the HCI general design problem and solution.

3. Conceptions/specifications of the HCI specific design problem and solution.

4. Strategy for developing HCI-EDPs.

5. Operationalisation/specifications of HCI specific design problems and solutions.

6.   Development cycle operationalisations.

7.   Evaluation/Testing procedure.

8.   Initial HCI-EDPs.

These claims are common, and so general, to the two case studies in the domains of application of the case studies. They demonstrate progress towards acquiring HCI-EDPs. The general progress comprises both the number of claims and their scope. All the critical outcomes, required for carry forward to future research, are included. The critical outcomes, listed as an ordered sequence are: acquisition of initial substantive HCI-EDPs (of some type), strategy for the development of such principles, cycle operationalisations to implement such a strategy, conceptions/specifications of general and specific design problems, and solutions to support such operationalisations and evaluation/testing to assess the solution of those general and specific problems.

10.2.2 FURTHER RESEARCH TOWARD ACQUIRING HCI ENGINEERING DESIGN PRINCIPLES

Both research case studies propose future research to acquire and to validate final, as opposed to intial, HCI-EDPs. These proposals are referenced for the application domain of domestic energy planning and control (§ 9.1) and for that of business-to-consumer electronic commerce (see § 9.2). The proposals are common to both domains of application and so can be considered general to them.

1. To develop further cycles of declarative and procedural initial HCI-EDPs.
2. To acquire final HCI-EDPs.
3. To develop the guarantee supporting HCI-EDPs.
4. To re-express HCI –EDPs in support of design practice.
5. To validate HCI-EDPs.

The proposals that are common, and so general, to the two domains of application demonstrate some consensus, concerning the research remaining to acquire and to validate complete HCI EDPs. The consensus comprises both the number of proposals and their scope. All the critical requirements for future research are included. The latter, as concern HCI-EDPs and listed in dependent order, are: development cycles, acquisition, guarantee development, and re-expression to support design and validation.

The proposals not common to the two domains of application derive essentially from the differences between the two domains themselves. Also, from the different strategies to acquire initial HCI-EDPs. The domestic energy planning and control case study employs a (primarily) bottom up, instance-first strategy to acquire initial such principles. The business-to-consumer electronic commerce case study employs a top down, clsas-first strategy to acquire initial such principles.

Although different, the case study proposals are necessarily complementary, because they both support the general proposal listing for HCI-EDP further research. So, for example, the domestic energy planning and control case study proposes to develop product and process tool support for MUSE/R in a manner comparable to the way in which the business-to-consumer electronic commerce case study proposes a method for specifying class design problem and class design solution and a method for specifying HCI-EDPs.

REVIEW

The chapter summarises the research progress towards HCI-EDPs for the two case studies in application domains of domestic energy planning and control and business-to-consumer electronic commerce. The progress common to both case studies is identified and so generalised over the two domains. The chapter then summarises the research remaining to acquire and to validate HCI-EDPs for both domains of application. The research remaining, common to both case studies, is identified and also generalised. The reasons for differences, particular to the case studies are identified and discussed

10.3   PRACTICE ASSIGNMENT

10.3.1   GENERAL
Read § 10.2.1.

- The claims of progress are listed only briefly, but sufficiently to support their identification. To ensure comprehension of the domestic energy planning and control and business-to-consumer electronic commerce concepts involved, for subsequent application to this and other domains, complete the following:

- Using § 9.1 and § 9.2, add details to the expression of the main concepts, as they relate to progress. The former can be at the same or at a lower level of description.

- Do you agree with the list of common progress claims for domestic energy planning and control and business-to-consumer electronic commerce? If not, using § 9.1 and § 9.2, delete those claims, with which you disagree and add those claims, with which you do agree. Rationalise any changes made.

Hints and Tips

Difficult to get started?

- Read the assignment tasks carefully.

- Make written notes, while re-reading § 10.2.1.

- Re-attempt the assignment.

Test

- Add further details to the expression of the progress claims from memory.

Read § 10.2.2.

The proposals for further research are listed briefly, but sufficiently to support their identification. To ensure comprehension of the domestic energy planning and control and business-to-consumer electronic commerce concepts involved, for subsequent application to this and other domains, complete the following.

- Using § 9.1 and § 9.2, add details to the expression of the main concepts, as they relate to further research. The former can be at the same or at a lower level of description.

- Do you agree with the list of the further research proposals for domestic energy planning and control and business-to-consumer electronic commerce? If not, using § 9.1 and § 9.22 delete those proposals, with which you disagree and add those proposals, with which you do agree. Rationalise any changes made.

Test

- Add further details to the expression of the proposals for research remaining from memory.

10.3.2 PRACTICE SCENARIOS

Practice Scenario 10.1 Applying Common Progress Claims to an Additional Domain of Application

Using the common progress claims of § 10.2.1, apply the main concepts listed to a novel domain of application other than domestic energy planning and control and business-to-consumer electronic commerce. The description can only be of the most general kind—that is at the level of the concepts listed. However, even consideration at this high level can orient the reader towards application of the concepts to novel domains of application. The latter are as might be required subsequently by their own work, that of their supervisor/instructor/teacher or that of another researcher. The practice scenario is intended to help bridge this gap.

Practice Scenario 10.2 Applying Further Research Proposals to an Additional Domain of Application

Using the further research proposals of § 10.2.2, apply the main concepts presented to a novel domain of application other than domestic energy planning and control and business-to-consumer electronic commerce. The description can only be of the most general kind—that is at the level of the concepts presented. However, even consideration at this high level can orient the reader towards application of the concepts to novel domains of application. The latter are as might be required subsequently by their own work, that of their supervisor/instructor/teacher or that of another researcher. The practice scenario is intended to help bridge this gap.

Postscript

The Preface makes clear the book's aims. It is now time to consider whether they have been met.

First, the scope and content of HCI design knowledge, for the purpose of acquiring initial HCI-EDPs, is characterised as craft artefacts and design practice experience, models and methods, and principles, rules, and heuristics. The latter characterisation reflects a discipline perspective and forms the basis of a critique of HCI design knowledge.

Second, the critique constitutes a challenge for HCI design knowledge of whatever sort, including that of HCI-EDPs, to provide more effective, that is reliable, support for HCI design practice.

Third, HCI-EDPs are proposed, as a way forward to meet the challenge of the greater reliability, required of HCI design knowledge, to support more effective HCI design practice.

Fourth, two case studies are summarised, which claim to have acquired initial, as opposed to final, HCI-EDPs for the application domains of domestic energy planning and control and of business-to-consumer electronic commerce.

Fifth and last, the claims of research progress, as concerns the acquisition of initial HCI-EDPs, are identified, along with the future research required for their final acquisition, operationalisation, test and generalisation, and so validation.

The book's aims, then, are considered to be met. This may sound immodest at first blush. However, the truth of the matter resides in the magnitude of the undertaking itself. It is clear that the progress is at best modest, compared with the longer-term research requirements to acquire and to validate final HCI EDPs. Perhaps a more realistic claim is that a start has been made. However, such a start is required to show explicitly whether HCI-EDPs are viable or not. This is a proper subject for HCI research.

Good luck to all who put forth and set sail on such a quest! They will need it.

Bibliography

Alexander, C. (1979). *The Timeless Way of Building*. UK: Oxford University Press. 88

Atwood, M., Gray, W., and John, B. (1996). Project Ernestine: analytic and empirical methods applied to a real world CHI Problem. In Rudisill, M., Lewis, C., Polson, P., and McKay, T. (Eds.), *Human Computer Interface Design: Success Stories, Emerging Methods and Real World Context*, p. 101. San Francisco, CA: Morgan Kaufmann. 91

Balaam, M., Comber, R., Jenkins, E., Sutton, S., and Garbett, A. (2015). FeedFinder: A location-mapping mobile application for breastfeeding women. *Proceedings CHI '15, 33rd Annual ACM*, p. 1709. Republic of Korea: ACM. DOI: 10.1145/2702123.2702328. 37

Barnard, P. (1991). Bridging between basic theories and the artifacts of human-computer interaction. In Carroll, J. (Ed.), *Designing Interaction*. UK: Cambridge University Press. 85

Baxter, G., Churchill, E., and Ritter, F. (2014). Addressing the fundamental error of design using the ABCS. *AIS SIGHCI Newsletter*, 13(1), 9-10. 111

Bayle, E. et al. (1997). Putting it all together: towards a pattern language for interaction design. *CHI'97 Worksh*op. 88

Bernard, M. (2002). Examining user expectations for the location of common e-commerce web objects. In *Usability News* 4.1, 2002. Retrieved on March 12, 2007 from http://psychology.wichita.edu/surl/usabilitynews/41/web_object-ecom.htm. 29

Bernard, M. and Sheshadri, A. (2004). Preliminary examination of global expectations of users' mental models for e-commerce web layouts. In *Usability News* 6.2, 2004. Retrieved on March 12, 2007 from http://psychology.wichita.edu/surl/usabilitynews/62/web_object_international.htm. 29

Bidigare, S. (2000). Information architecture of the shopping cart. *Argus Centre for Information Architecture White Paper*. 29, 77

Camara, F. and Calvary, G. (2017). Bringing worth maps a step further: a dedicated on-line resource. *Human-Computer Interaction – Interact 2017*. Bernhaupt, R., Dalvi, G., Joshi, A., Balkrishan, D., O'Neill, J., and Winckler, M. (Eds.), LNCS 10515 Springer 95-113. DOI: 10.1007/978-3-319-67687-6_8. 16, 35

Card, S., Moran, T., and Newell, A. (1983). *The Psychology of Human-Computer Interaction*. Hillsdale, NJ: LEA. 50, 85, 91

Carroll, J. (2003). Introduction: Toward a multidisciplinary science of human-computer interaction. In Carroll, J. (Ed.), *HCI Models, Theories and Frameworks*. San Francisco, CA: Morgan Kaufmann. DOI: 10.1016/B978-155860808-5/50001-0. 36, 52, 56, 61, 86, 112, 113

Carroll, J. (2010). Conceptualizing A Possible Discipline Of Human-Computer Interaction. *Interacting with Computers*, 22(1), 3-12. DOI: 10.1016/j.intcom.2009.11.008. 36, 52, 56, 61, 86, 112, 113

Carroll, J., Kellog, W., and Rosson, M. (1991). The task-artifact cycle in designing interaction. In Carroll, J. (Ed.), *Designing Interaction*. Cambridge, UK: Cambridge University Press. 52

Chaparro, B. (2001). Top ten mistakes of shopping cart design. *Internet Working*, 4.1. 29, 52, 77

Cockton, G. (2009). Getting there: Six meta-principles and interaction design. In *CHI '09 Proceedings of the SIGCHI Conference on Human Factors in Computing Systems*. April 2009, pp. 2223-2232. DOI: 10.1145/1518701.1519041. 84

Cummaford, S. (2000). Validating effective design knowledge for re-use: HCI engineering design principles. In *CHI '00 Extended Abstracts on Human Factors in Computing Systems*. New York: ACM Press. DOI: 10.1145/633292.633336. 88

Cummaford, S. (2007). HCI engineering design principles: Acquisition of class-level knowledge. Unpublished Ph.D. Thesis, University of London. xix, 20, 26, 92, 103, 104, 106, 107, 108

Cummaford, S. and Long, J. (1998). Towards a conception of HCI engineering design principles. In *Proceedings of Ninth European Conference on Cognitive Ergonomics (ECCE9)*, Limerick, Ireland. 88, 91

Cummaford, S. and Long, J. (1999). Costs matrix: Systematic comparisons of competing design solutions. In *Proceedings INTERACT 99, Volume II*, Edinburgh UK, Aug 39–Sept 3, 1999.

Da Silva, T., Silveira, F., Silveira M., Hellmann, T., and Maurer, F. (2015). A systematic mapping on agile UCD across the major agile and HCI conferences. In *Proceedings ICCSA* 2015, Banff, AB Canada. DOI: 10.1007/978-3-319-21413-9_7. 4, 111

Denley, I. and Long, J. (2001). Multi-disciplinary practice in requirements engineering: problems and criteria for support. In Blandford, A., Vanderdonkt, J., and Gray, P. (Eds.), *People and Computers XV – Interaction without Frontiers. Joint proceedings of HCI 2001 and IHM 2001*. London: Springer Verlag. DOI: 10.1007/978-1-4471-0353-0_8. 54

Dowell, J. (1998). Formulating the cognitive design problem of air traffic management. *International Journal of Human-Computer Studies*, 49(5), 743-766. DOI: 10.1006/ijhc.1998.0225. 56, 61, 110, 112

Dowell J. and Long J. (1989). Towards a conception for an engineering discipline of human factors. *Ergonomics*, 32(11), 1513-1535. DOI: 10.1080/00140138908966921. 52, 56, 57, 86, 87, 89, 90, 93, 95, 96

Gamma, E., Helm, R., Johnson, R., and Vlissides, J. (1995). *Design Patterns, Elements of Reusable Object-Oriented Software*. US: Addison-Wesley Publishing Company. 88

Glaser, B. and Strauss, A. (1967). *Discovery of Grounded Theory*. London: Aldine. 53, 54

Gothelf, J. and Seiden, J. (2016). *Lean UX – Designing Great Products with Agile Teams*. US: O'Reilly Media Inc. 4

Harper, R., Rodden, T., Rogers, Y., and Sellen, A. (2008). *Being Human – Human-Computer Interaction in the Year 2020*. Cambridge, UK: Microsoft Research Ltd. 3, 8

Hartson, R. and Pyla, P. (2018). *The UX Book: Agile UX Design for a Quality User Experience*. US: Morgan Kaufman. xix, 14, 20, 22, 26, 30

Hevner, A., Ram, S., March, S., and Park, J. (2004) Design science in information systems research, *MIS Quarterly*, 28(1), 75-105. DOI: 10.2307/25148625. 4, 20, 26, 111

Hill, B. (2010). Diagnosing co-ordination problems in the emergency management response to disasters. *Interacting with Computers*, 22(1), 43-55. DOI: 10.1016/j.intcom.2009.11.003. 57, 58 , 61, 110, 112

John, B. and Gray, W. (1995). CPM-GOMS: An analysis method for tasks with parallel activities. In *Conference Companion on Human Factors in Computing Systems CHI'95*, ACM. DOI: 10.1145/223355.223738. 51, 91

Kalakota,R and Whinston, A. (1996). *Frontiers of Electronic Commerce*. US: Addison Wesley Longman Publishing Co., Inc. DOI: 10.1109/TCPMC.1996.507151. 104

Kienan, T. (2001). Boosting transaction usability. Tauberkienen Transaction Systems Report. 29, 77

Kim, G. (2020). *Human-Computer Interaction - Fundamentals and Practice*. UK: CRC Press, Taylor and Francis. xix, 35

Kirsh, D. (2001). The context of work. *HCI*, 6(2), 306–322. DOI: 10.1207/S15327051HCI16234_12. 51

Lim K. and Long, J. (1994). *The MUSE Method for Usability Engineering*. Cambridge, UK: Cambridge University Press. DOI: 10.1017/CBO9780511624230. 27, 38, 53, 54, 55, 91, 96, 112

Long, J. (2010). Some celebratory reflections on a celebratory hci festschrift, *Interacting with Computers*, 22(1), 68-71. DOI: 10.1016/j.intcom.2009.11.006. xix, 91

Long, J. (2021). *Approaches and Frameworks for HCI Research*. Cambridge: Cambridge University Press. DOI: 10.1017/9781108754972. xix, 3, 4, 7, 13, 14, 19, 25, 35, 49, 84, 90, 91, 112, 113

Long, J. and Brostoff, S. (2002). Validating design knowledge in the home: a successful case-study of dementia care. In Reed, D., Baxter, G., and Blythe, M. (Eds.), *EACE '12*. France: European Association of Cognitive Ergonomics. 91

Long, J. and Dowell, J. (1989). Conceptions of the discipline of HCI: Craft, applied science and engineering. In Sutcliffe, A. and Macaulay, L. (Eds.), *People and Computers V*. Cambridge, UK: Cambridge University Press. 52, 56, 57, 86, 95

Long, J. and Hill, B. (2005). Validating diagnostic design knowledge for air traffic management: a case-study. In Marmaras, N., Kontogiannis, T. and Nathanael, D. (Eds.), *EACE '05*. Greece: European Association of Cognitive Ergonomics. 91, 112

Long, J. and Monk, A. (2002). Applying an engineering framework to telemedical research: a successful case-study. In Khalid, H. and Helander, M. (Eds.), *Proceedings of 7th International Conference on Working with Computers*. Kuala Lumpur, Malaysia. 91

Long, J., Cummaford, S., and Stork, A. (2022, in press). *Towards Engineering Design Principles for HCI*. Switzerland: Springer Nature. x, xvii, xviii, xix, 3, 9, 13, 14, 19, 20, 25, 26, 35, 49, 65, 83, 88, 90, 95, 111, 113

Morton, J., Barnard, P., Hammond, N., and Long, J. (1979). Interacting with the computer: A framework. In Boutmy, E. and Danthine, A., (Eds.), *Teleinformatics '79*. Amsterdam: North Holland. 50

Nielsen, J. (1993). *Usability Engineering*. San Francisco: Morgan Kaufman. DOI: 10.1016/B978-0-08-052029-2.50007-3. 71

Nielsen, J. (1994a). Enhancing the explanatory power of usability heuristics. *Proceedings ACM CHI'94 Conference* (Boston, MA, April, 24-28), pp. 152-158. DOI: 10.1145/259963.260333. 71

Nielsen, J. (1994b). Heuristic evaluation. In Nielsen, J., and Mack, R. (Eds.), *Usability Methods*. New York, NY: John Wiley & Sons. 71

Norman, D. (1983). Design principles for human-computer interfaces. In Smith, R., Pew, R. and Janda, A. (Eds.), *Proceedings of CHI 83, Human Factors in Computing Systems Conference*. Boston, MA: U.S. ACM. DOI: 10.1145/800045.801571. 68

Norman, D. (1986). Cognitive engineering. In Draper, S. and Norman, D. (Eds.), *User Centred System Design*. Hillsdale, NJ: Lawrence Erlbaum Associates. 68

Norman, D. (2010). The transmedia design challenge: Technology that is pleasurable and satisfying. *Interactions*, 17(1), 12-15. DOI: 10.1145/1649475.1649478. 77

Norman, D. (2013). *The Design of Everyday Things* (Revised Ed.). NY: Basic Books. 68, 77, 86, 111

Pew, R. and Mavor, A. (2007). *Human-System Integration in the System Development Process – A New Look*. US: The National Academies Press. 94

Rauterberg, M. (2006). HCI as an engineering discipline: To be or not to be!? *African Journal of Information and Communication Technology*, 2(4), 163-184. DOI: 10.5130/ajict.v2i4.365. 61, 86

Ritter, F., Baxter, G., and Churchill, E. (2014). *User-Centred Systems Design – A Brief History in Foundations for Designing User-Centered Systems*, pp. 33-54. Switzerland: Springer Nature. DOI: 10.1007/978-1-4471-5134-0. xix, 14, 22, 30

Roedl, D. and Stolterman, E. (2013). Design research at CHI and its applicability to design practice. In *Proceedings ACM CHI'13 Conference on Human Factors in Computing Systems*, 1951-1954. DOI: 10.1145/2470654.2466257. 4, 43, 111

Rogers, Y. (2012). *HCI Theory - Classical, Modern, and Contemporary*. UK: Morgan and Claypool. DOI: 10.2200/S00418ED1V01Y201205HCI014. 4, 6, 10, 14, 85, 90

Rogers, Y., Sharp, H., and Preece, J. (2011). *Interaction Design: Beyond Human- Computer Interaction*, 3rd ed. Chichester: John Wiley and Sons Ltd. 3, 8, 50, 53, 55, 63, 77

Seffah, A. (2015). *Patterns of HCI Design and HCI Design of Patterns*. Switzerland: Springer Nature. DOI: 10.1007/978-3-319-15687-3. 88

Sharp, H., Rogers, Y., and Preece, J. (2007). *Interaction Design: Beyond Human-Computer Interaction*, 2nd. ed. Chichester, England: John Wiley and Sons Ltd. 8

Shneiderman, B. (1983). Direct manipulation: A step beyond programming languages. *IEEE Computer*, 16(8), 57. DOI: 10.1109/MC.1983.1654471. 27, 70

Shneiderman, B. (1998). *Designing the User Interface: Strategies for Effective Human- Computer Interaction*, 3rd ed. Reading, MA: Addison-Wesley. 70, 85

Shneiderman, B. (2010). *Designing the User Interface: Strategies for Effective Human- Computer Interaction*, 5th Edition. Reading, MA: Addison-Wesley. 27, 54, 77

Shneiderman, B. and Plaisant, E. (2004). Strategies for evaluating information visualization tools: Multi-dimensional in-depth long-term case studies. *Conference: Proceedings of the 2006 Avi Workshop on Beyond Time and Errors: Novel Evaluation Methods for Information Visualization. Beliv 2006*, Venice, Italy, May 23, 2006. DOI: 10.1145/1168149.1168158. 77

Smith, M. and Mosier, J. (1986). Guidelines for designing interface software. Mitre Corporation Report MTR9240 Mitre Corporation. DOI: 10.21236/ADA177198. 27

Smith, W., Hill, B., Long, J., and Whitefield, A. (1997). A design-oriented framework for modelling the planning and control of multiple task work in secretarial office administration. *Behaviour & Information Technology*, 16(3), 289-309. DOI: 10.1080/014492997119897. 51, 110

Snow Valley (2005a). Part 1: Transactional navigation elements style and terminology. IMRG E-retail Standardisation Report. 29

Snow Valley Report (2005b). Part 2: The checkout process. IMRG E-retail Standardisation Report. 29 , 30

Stork, A. (1999). Towards Engineering Principles for Human-Computer Interaction (Domestic Energy Planning and Control). Unpublished Ph.D. Thesis, University of London. xix, 14, 26, 88, 92, 96, 97, 98, 99

Teo, L. and John, B. (2008). CogTool-Explorer: Towards a tool for predicting user interaction. In *Proceedings CHI EA'08*, ACM, pp. 2793–2798. DOI: 10.1145/1358628.1358763. 51

Timmer, P. and Long, J. (2002). Expressing the effectiveness of planning horizons. *Le Travail Humain*, 65(2), 103-126. DOI: 10.3917/th.652.0103. 52, 53, 61, 76, 91, 110

Walsh, I. (2003). Good information architecture increases online sales. Sitepoint, October 23, 2003. 29, 77

Watts, L. and Monk, A. (1997). Telemedical consultation: Task characteristics. In *Proceedings CHI '97*, Atlanta, Georgia. ACM Press, pp. 534-535. DOI: 10.1145/258549.259013. 91

Watts, L. and Monk, A. (1998). Reasoning about tasks, activity and technology to support collaboration. *Ergonomics*, 41(11), 1583-1606. DOI: 10.1080/001401398186081. 91

Wickens, D. (1984). *Engineering Psychology and Human Performance*. Columbus: Merrill. 66

Wickens, D. (1993) Cognitive factors in display design. *Journal of the Washington Academy of Sciences*, 83(4), 179-201. 66

Wickens, C., Lee, J., and Becker, G. (2004). *An Introduction to Human Factors Engineering*, 2nd ed., Pearson 2004, Ch. 8. 76, 86, 111

Wright, P., Fields, R., and Harrison, M. (2000). Analysing human-computer interaction as distributed cognition: The resources model. *Human Computer Interaction*, 51(1), 1–41. DOI: 10.1207/S15327051HCI1501_01. 51

Zagalo, N. (2020). *Engagement Design: Designing for Interaction Motivations*. Switzerland: Springer Nature. DOI: 10.1007/978-3-030-37085-5. xix, 14, 22, 30, 36

Authors' Biographies

John Long

University Degrees

M.A. Modern Languages (Cambridge), B.Sc. Psychology (Hull), Ph.D. (Cambridge) and D.Sc. (London).

Books/Theses

Multidimensional Signal Recognition: Reduced Efficiency and Process Interaction (Ph.D.), *Attention and Performance IX*, with Alan Baddeley (LEA), *Cognitive Ergonomics and Human-Computer Interaction*, with Andy Whitefield (CUP), *The MUSE Method for Usability Engineering*, with Kee Yong Lim (CUP), *Approaches and Frameworks for HCI Research*, (CUP), and *Towards Engineering Design Principles for HCI*, with Steve Cummaford and Adam Stork (Springer Nature).

Steve Cummaford

University Degrees

B.A. Philosophy (York), M.Sc. Cognitive Science (Cardiff), Ph.D. (London).

Books/Theses

The Effects of Expected and Unexpected Interruptions on Completion of Computer-based Tasks (M.Sc. Thesis), HCI Engineering Design Principles: Acquisition of Class-Level Knowledge (Ph.D.), and *Towards Engineering Design Principles for HCI*, with John Long and Adam Stork (M&C).

Current Position

Lead digital product designer at Ted Baker

Adam Stork

University Degrees

B.Sc. Computing and Robotics (Kent), M.Sc. Ergonomics/Human-Computer Interaction (London), and Ph.D. (London).

Books/Theses

A Formal Description of Worksystem Behaviours and Interactions (M.Sc. Thesis), Towards Engineering Principles for Human-Computer Interaction (Ph.D.) and

Towards Engineering Design Principles for HCI, with John Long and Steve Cummaford, (M&C).

Current Position

Partner, also strategy and transformation consultant at Concerto.